Generalist Practice with Organizations and Communities

Karen K. Kirst-Ashman

University of Wisconsin, Whitewater

Grafton H. Hull, Jr.

University of Utah

Prepared by

Vicki Vogel

University of Wisconsin, Whitewater

BROOKS/COLE
CENGAGE Learning™

Australia • Brazil • Japan • Korea • Mexico • Singapore • Spain • United Kingdom • United States

For product information and technology assistance, contact us at **Cengage Learning Customer & Sales Support, 1-800-354-9706**

For permission to use material from this text or product, submit all requests online at **www.cengage.com/permissions** Further permissions questions can be emailed to **permissionrequest@cengage.com**

ISBN-13: 978-0-8400-3463-2
ISBN-10: 0-8400-3463-6

Brooks/Cole Cengage Learning
20 Davis Drive
Belmont, CA 94002-3098
USA

Cengage Learning is a leading provider of customized learning solutions with office locations around the globe, including Singapore, the United Kingdom, Australia, Mexico, Brazil, and Japan. Locate your local office at: **www.cengage.com/global**

Cengage Learning products are represented in Canada by Nelson Education, Ltd.

To learn more about Brooks/Cole, visit **www.cengage.com/brookscole**

Purchase any of our products at your local college store or at our preferred online store **www.cengagebrain.com**

Printed in the United States of America
2 3 4 5 6   18 17 16 15 14

Dear Social Work Student,

Welcome to *Competencies/Practice Behaviors Workbook* for Kirst-Ashman/Hull's *Generalist Practice with Organizations and Communities*, 5e. Throughout your course you will acquire a great deal of new knowledge, including an introduction to new theories, informative research, and practical skills like critical thinking skills and frameworks for appreciating and overcoming challenges. All of the knowledge you gain will offer you a deeper, richer understanding of social work. Used in conjunction with your text and other resources, the *Competencies/Practice Behaviors Workbook* presents you with Practice Exercises that will teach you how to transform your new knowledge into social work Practice Behaviors.

About Competence and Practice Behavior
In social work, the words Competence and Practice Behavior have a unique meaning beyond the typical dictionary definitions. "Competence" in the usual sense means that a person possesses suitable skills and abilities to do a specific task. A competent baseball player must move quickly, catch, throw, and play as part of a team. They also have to think quickly, understand the rules of the game, and be knowledgeable of their environment. In the same way, a competent social worker should be able to do a number of job-related duties, think critically, and understand the context of their work. The Council on Social Work Education (CSWE) has defined specific Core Competency areas for all social work students, and their corresponding Practice Behaviors as follows:

Competencies and Practice Behaviors
2.1.1 Identify as a Professional Social Worker and Conduct Oneself Accordingly
a. Advocate for client access to the services of social work
b. Practice personal reflection and self-correction to assure continual professional development
c. Attend to professional roles and boundaries
d. Demonstrate professional demeanor in behavior, appearance, and communication
e. Engage in career-long learning
f. Use supervision and consultation
2.1.2 Apply Social Work Ethical Principles to Guide Professional Practice
a. Recognize and manage personal values in a way that allows professional values to guide practice
b. Make ethical decisions by applying standards of the National Association of Social Workers Code of Ethics and, as applicable, of the International Federation of Social Workers/ International Association of Schools of Social Work Ethics in Social Work, Statement of Principles

c.	Tolerate ambiguity in resolving ethical conflicts
d.	Apply strategies of ethical reasoning to arrive at principled decisions

2.1.3 Apply Critical Thinking to Inform and Communicate Professional Judgments

a.	Distinguish, appraise, and integrate multiple sources of knowledge, including research-based knowledge and practice wisdom
b.	Analyze models of assessment, prevention, intervention, and evaluation
c.	Demonstrate effective oral and written communication in working with individuals, families, groups, organizations, communities, and colleagues

2.1.4 Engage Diversity and Difference in Practice

a.	Recognize the extent to which a culture's structures and values may oppress, marginalize, alienate, or create or enhance privilege and power
b.	Gain sufficient self-awareness to eliminate the influence of personal biases and values in working with diverse groups
c.	Recognize and communicate their understanding of the importance of difference in shaping life experiences
d.	View themselves as learners and engage those with whom they work as informants

2.1.5 Advance Human Rights and Social and Economic Justice

a.	Understand the forms and mechanisms of oppression and discrimination
b.	Advocate for human rights and social and economic justice
c.	Engage in practices that advance social and economic justice

2.1.6 Engage in Research-Informed Practice and Practice-Informed Research

a.	Use practice experience to inform scientific inquiry
b.	Use research evidence to inform practice

2.1.7 Apply Knowledge of Human Behavior and the Social Environment

a.	Utilize conceptual frameworks to guide the processes of assessment, intervention, and evaluation
b.	Critique and apply knowledge to understand person and environment

2.1.8 Engage in Policy Practice to Advance Social and Economic Well-Being and to Deliver Effective Social Work Services

a.	Analyze, formulate, and advocate for policies that advance social well-being
b.	Collaborate with colleagues and clients for effective policy action

2.1.9 Respond to Contexts that Shape Practice

a.	Continuously discover, appraise, and attend to changing locales, populations, scientific and technological developments, and emerging societal trends to provide relevant services
b.	Provide leadership in promoting sustainable changes in service delivery and practice to improve the quality of social services

2.1.10 Engage, Assess, Intervene, and Evaluate with Individuals, Families, Groups, Organizations and Communities

a.	Substantively and affectively prepare for action with individuals, families, groups, organizations, and communities
b.	Use empathy and other interpersonal skills
c.	Develop a mutually agreed-on focus of work and desired outcomes
d.	Collect, organize, and interpret client data
e.	Assess client strengths and limitations

f.	Develop mutually agreed-on intervention goals and objectives
g.	Select appropriate intervention strategies
h.	Initiate actions to achieve organizational goals
i.	Implement prevention interventions that enhance client capacities
j.	Help clients resolve problems
k.	Negotiate, mediate, and advocate for clients
l.	Facilitate transitions and endings
m.	Critically analyze, monitor, and evaluate interventions

Each of the Exercises in the *Practice Behaviors Workbook* will focus on learning and applying social work Practice Behaviors. While every Exercise will not ask you to apply Competencies or Practice Behaviors from every Core Competency area, by the time you finish your course you will have practiced many and gained a better working knowledge of how social work is done. The goal, shared by your professors, your program, the authors of this text, and by Brooks/Cole, Cengage Learning Social Work team, is that by the end of your curriculum you will have honed your Practice Behaviors in all of the Core Competency areas into a skill set that empowers you to work effectively as a professional social worker.

Assessing Competence: Partnering with Your Instructor and Peer Evaluator
As described above, the Council on Social Work Education clearly defines the Competencies and Practice Behaviors that a social work student should be trained to employ. Therefore, the grading rubric that comes at the end of every chapter of the *Practice Behaviors Workbook* is adapted from Competencies and Practice Behaviors defined by CSWE (see the table above). To assess your competence during your course, we recommend you partner with a peer(s) who can act as your course "evaluator(s)" to genuinely assess both your written assignments and your role-plays; be sure to ask your professor to comment on and approve the assessments once they are completed by you and your Evaluator. It is our hope that partnering with your classmates in this way will familiarize you with the unique learning opportunity you will have in your Field Experience – the signature pedagogy of social work education. There you will apply all of your knowledge and skills under the supervision of your Field Instructor and Field Liaison before completing your required curriculum.

As always, we thank you for your commitment to education and to the profession. Enjoy your course, and *feel empowered to help others*!

Contents

Competencies/Practice Behaviors Exercise 1.1
What Does Generalist Practice Mean?

Focus Competencies or Practice Behaviors:
- EP 2.1.7a   Utilize conceptual frameworks to guide the process of assessment, intervention, and evaluation

Instructions:
A.   Review the following outline of the definition of generalist practice
B.   Describe why each concept is important to social work, and to your professional identity as a social worker

---

AN OUTLINE OF THE DEFINITION OF GENERALIST PRACTICE

1.   **Acquisition of an eclectic knowledge base**
    A.   Theoretical foundation: Systems theories
    B.   Human behavior and the social environment
    C.   Social welfare policy and policy practice
    D.   Social work practice
    E.   Research
    F.   Values and principles that guide practice
2.   **Acquisition of professional values and application of professional ethics**
    A.   National Association of Social Workers Code of Ethics
    B.   International Federation of Social Workers/International Association of Schools of Social Work Ethics in Social Work, Statement of Principles
    C.   Awareness of personal values
    D.   Management of ethical dilemmas
3.   **Use of a wide range or practice skills**
    A.   Micro
    B.   Mezzo
    C.   Macro
4.   **Orientation to target any size system**
    A.   Micro
    B.   Mezzo
    C.   Macro
5.   **Emphasis on client empowerment, strengths and resiliency**
6.   **The importance of human diversity**
7.   **Advocacy for human rights, and the pursuit of social and economic justice**
8.   **Effective work within an organizational structure**
9.   **Assumption of a wide range of professional roles**
    A.   Enabler
    B.   Mediator
    C.   Integrator/Coordinator
    D.   Manager
    E.   Educator
    F.   Analyst/Evaluator
    G.   Broker

	H.	Facilitator
	I.	Initiator
	J.	Negotiator
	K.	Mobilizer
	L.	Advocate
10.	**Employment of critical thinking skills**	
11.	**Research-informed practice**	
12.	**Use of the planned change process**	

Competencies/Practice Behaviors Exercise 1.2
Critical Thinking Skills: Finding Fallacies

Focus Competencies or Practice Behaviors:
- EP 2.1.3   Apply critical thinking to inform and communicate professional judgments

Instructions:
A.   Use critical thinking to identify fallacies in the case scenarios below, then describe why you came to that conclusion

Scenario A:
Re-Elect the Mayor:
Your mayor states that you and other citizens should trust in his good judgment about how to allocate the city's resources, although he does not as yet have a detailed plan or budget in place. He stresses that this is his second term in office and he has a sound track record for making decisions in the past. He mentions that the major newspaper in town consistently supports him and his decisions.

Fallacy: _____

_____

Why: _____

_____

Scenario B:
A Famous Expert:
You are a social worker in a county department of social services. Your colleague Allison has just attended a seminar presented by Dr. B.S. Smock, a renowned expert in radical approaches to crisis intervention. This expert has published two books and several articles on the subject. Allison vehemently states that she thinks all the agency workers should be trained in Dr. Smock's techniques and use his suggestions. She indicates that several clients spoke at the seminar and provided testimony concerning the effectiveness of the approach. Allison is clearly a loyal and enthusiastic disciple of Dr. Smock.

Fallacy: _____

_____

Why: _____

_____

Scenario C:
Advice from a Colleague:
"I've had the best luck with the Gung-ho Intervention technique on Ollie Hopnoodle. I'm going to use it with all my clients. I think the whole agency should adopt it."

Fallacy: _____

Why: _____
_____

Scenario D:
The Wave of the Future:
"Absolute Attainment Management is the wave of the future. It beats everything about the old bureaucratic approach to running social service organizations. Every in-the-know agency is starting to use it. Let's go for it! We don't want to be left behind."

Fallacy: _____

Why: _____
_____

Scenario E:
Moneyplenty:
"I heard Ernie over at Moneyplenty Mental Health Center absolutely rave about their grant-writing seminars. I've got to get myself enrolled – but the fee is about 750 big ones. Do you think the agency might pay for at least half?"

Fallacy: _____

Why: _____
_____

Competencies/Practice Behaviors Exercise 1.3
Roles in Macro Practice

Focus Competencies or Practice Behaviors:
- EP 2.1.1c   Apply critical thinking to inform and communicate professional judgments

Instructions:

A.   Cite which social work macro practice roles (enabler, mediator, integrator/coordinator, manager, educator, analyst/evaluator, broker, facilitator, initiator, negotiator, mobilizer, and advocate) are utilized in the following scenarios. See your text for a description of each role

B.   Explain how each role functions in these scenarios

Scenario A:
Creating Communication Channels:
A social worker employed by a neighborhood center determines that the various workers and other professionals dealing with adolescent clients are not communicating with each other. For example, school social workers have no established procedure for conveying information to protective services workers who, in turn, do not communicate readily with probation and parole workers—despite the fact that these professionals are working with many of the same clients. The neighborhood center social worker decides to bring together representatives from the various agencies that serve the center and establish more clearly defined communication channels.

Macro Practice Role(s):

_____

_____

Explanation:

_____

_____

Scenario B:
Peer Trainings:
A worker in a Child Protective Services Unit has developed special skills in family counseling by participating in a two-year training program. Her agency's Assistant Director asks her to provide a series of six in-service training program for other Child Protective Services staff.[1]

Macro Practice Role(s):

_____

_____

Explanation:

_____

_____

Scenario C:
Improving Agency Service Provision:
The main tasks of a Foster Care Unit are to assess potential foster parent applicants, monitor placement, manage cases as children move in and out of foster care, and train foster parents in parenting and behavior-management skills. The unit social workers hold biweekly meetings to discuss how to improve agency service provision. The workers take turns organizing the meetings and running the discussions.

Macro Practice Role(s):

_____

_____

Explanation:

_____

_____

---

[1] *In-service training programs* are educational sessions provided by an agency for its staff to develop their skills or improve their effectiveness.

4

Scenario D:

A System of Assessment and Referral:

A social worker employed by a large private family services agency specializes in international adoptions, especially those involving countries from Northeastern Europe, Central Asia, and China. He discovers that many of the adoptive children suffer from health problems caused by early nutritional deprivation. The worker is convinced that this is not a matter of one or two problem cases, but a disturbing pattern. No automatic referral process is in place to assess these adoptive children and direct their families to needed resources, including designated medical specialists. The worker devises a systematic process for assessment and referral.

Macro Practice Role(s):

_____

_____

Explanation:

_____

_____

Scenario E:

Assessment of Services:

Agency administration asks one of three social workers in a large residential health care complex for older adults to assess the effectiveness of its social services program.

Macro Practice Role(s):

_____

_____

Explanation:

_____

_____

Competencies/Practice Behaviors Exercise 1.4
Dynamic Case Role Play

Focus Competencies or Practice Behaviors:
- EP 2.1.10a   Substantively and affectively prepare for action with individuals, families, groups, organizations, and communities

Instructions:

A.   In **Exercise 1.3 Scenario A:** "Creating Communication Channels," you matched some typical social work scenarios to the appropriate social work practice roles and explained how the roles were relevant. In this exercise, you and a partner will role play one of those scenarios. Utilize the description of the Macro Practice Roles, whether it is enabler, mediator, integrator/coordinator, manager, educator, analyst/evaluator, broker, facilitator, initiator, negotiator, mobilizer, and/or advocate, and take turns acting as Evaluator for each other. Be sure to note your evaluations on the Competencies/Practice Behaviors Exercises Assessment form at the end of this chapter.

Scenario:

A social worker employed by a neighborhood center determines that the various workers and other professionals dealing with adolescent clients are not communicating with each other. For example, school social workers have no established procedure for conveying information to protective services workers who, in turn, do not communicate readily with probation and parole workers—despite the fact that these professionals are working with many of the same clients. The neighborhood center social worker decides to bring together representatives from the various agencies that serve the center and establish more clearly defined communication channels.

You are the worker presenting this idea to your Social Work Supervisor. Describe how you will set up the meeting and how you will meet – in person, by email, or with a teleconference? What information will you need to gather before the meeting? What information do you hope to get from the participants during the meeting? What actions will you ask the attendees to take after the meeting?

Case Scenario Notes:

Chapter 1 Competencies/Practice Behaviors Exercises Assessment:

Name: _____ **Date:** _____

Supervisor's Name: _____

Focus Competencies/Practice Behaviors:
- EP 2.1.1c   Attend to professional roles and boundaries
- EP 2.1.3   Apply critical thinking to inform and communicate professional judgments
- EP 2.1.7a   Utilize conceptual frameworks to guide the processes of assessment, intervention, and evaluation
- EP 2.1.10a   Substantively and affectively prepare for action with individuals, families, groups, organizations, and communities

Instructions:

A.   Evaluate your work or your partner's work in the Focus Competencies/Practice Behaviors by completing the Competencies/Practice Behaviors Assessment form below

B.   What other Competencies/Practice Behaviors did you use to complete these Exercises? Be sure to record them in your assessments

1.	I have attained this competency/practice behavior (in the range of 81 to 100%)
2.	I have largely attained this competency/practice behavior (in the range of 61 to 80%)
3.	I have partially attained this competency/practice behavior (in the range of 41 to 60%)
4.	I have made a little progress in attaining this competency/practice behavior (in the range of 21 to 40%)
5.	I have made almost no progress in attaining this competency/practice behavior (in the range of 0 to 20%)

EPAS 2008 Core Competencies & Core Practice Behaviors							Student Self Assessment	Evaluator Feedback
Student and Evaluator Assessment Scale and Comments	0	1	2	3	4	5		Agree/Disagree/Comments
EP 2.1.1 Identity as a Professional Social Worker and Conduct Oneself Accordingly:								
a. Advocate for client access to the services of social work								
b. Practice personal reflection and self-correction to assure continual professional development								
c. Attend to professional roles and boundaries								
d. Demonstrate professional demeanor in behavior, appearance, and communication								
e. Engage in career-long learning								
f. Use supervision and consultation								
EP 2.1.2 Apply Social Work Ethical Principles to Guide Professional Practice:								
a. Recognize and manage personal values in a way that allows professional values to guide practice								
b. Make ethical decisions by applying NASW Code of Ethics and, as applicable, of the IFSW/IASSW Ethics in Social Work, Statement of Principles								
c. Tolerate ambiguity in resolving ethical conflicts								
d. Apply strategies of ethical reasoning to arrive at principled decisions								

EP 2.1.3 Apply Critical Thinking to Inform and Communicate Professional Judgments:						
a. Distinguish, appraise, and integrate multiple sources of knowledge, including research-based knowledge and practice wisdom						
b. Analyze models of assessment, prevention, intervention, and evaluation						
c. Demonstrate effective oral and written communication in working with individuals, families, groups, organizations, communities, and colleagues						
EP 2.1.4 Engage Diversity and Difference in Practice:						
a. Recognize the extent to which a culture's structures and values may oppress, marginalize, alienate, or create or enhance privilege and power						
b. Gain sufficient self-awareness to eliminate the influence of personal biases and values in working with diverse groups						
c. Recognize and communicate their understanding of the importance of difference in shaping life experiences						
d. View themselves as learners and engage those with whom they work as informants						
EP 2.1.5 Advance Human Rights and Social and Economic Justice						
a. Understand forms and mechanisms of oppression and discrimination						
b. Advocate for human rights and social and economic justice						
c. Engage in practices that advance social and economic justice						
EP 2.1.6 Engage in Research-informed Practice and Practice-Informed Research						
a. Use practice experience to inform scientific inquiry						
b. Use research evidence to inform practice						
EP 2.1.7 Apply Knowledge of Human Behavior and the Social Environment:						
a. Utilize conceptual frameworks to guide the processes of assessment, intervention, and evaluation						
b. Critique and apply knowledge to understand person and environment						
EP 2.1.8 Engage in Policy Practice to Advance Social and Economic Well-being and to Deliver Effective Social Work Services:						
a. Analyze, formulate, and advocate for policies that advance social well-being						
b. Collaborate with colleagues and clients for effective policy action						
EP 2.1.9 Respond to Contexts that Shape Practice:						
a. Continuously discover, appraise, and attend to changing locales, populations, scientific and technological developments, and emerging societal trends to provide relevant services						
b. Provide leadership in promoting sustainable changes in service delivery and practice to improve the quality of social services						

EP 2.1.10 Engage, Assess, Intervene, and Evaluate with Individuals, Families, Groups, Organizations and Communities:							
a. Substantively and affectively prepare for action with individuals, families, groups, organizations, and communities							
b. Use empathy and other interpersonal skills							
c. Develop a mutually agreed-on focus of work and desired outcomes							
d. Collect, organize, and interpret client data							
e. Assess client strengths and limitations							
f. Develop mutually agreed-on intervention goals and objectives							
g. Select appropriate intervention strategies.							
h. Initiate actions to achieve organizational goals							
i. Implement prevention interventions that enhance client capacities							
j. Help clients resolve problems							
k. Negotiate, mediate, and advocate for clients							
l. Facilitate transitions and endings							
m. Critically analyze, monitor, and evaluate interventions							

Competencies/Practice Behaviors Exercise 2.1
Practicing Empathic Responses in Macro Practice Contexts

Focus Competencies or Practice Behaviors:
- EP 2.1.10b   Use empathy and other interpersonal skills

Instructions:

A.   Review the content on empathy (*empathy* is not only being in tune with how other people feel, but also conveying to people both verbally and nonverbally that you understand how they feel)

B.   Read the following vignettes and propose two empathic responses for each situation

C.   **Vignette #1 provides an example**

Vignette #1: You are a school social worker in an urban neighborhood. Residents inform you that a vacant lot in the neighborhood—two houses away from the school—was used as a dump for dangerous chemicals between ten and twenty years ago. In the past fifteen years, a dozen children attending the school have gotten cancer.

Addressing this type of issue is not part of your job description, but you see it as your professional and ethical responsibility to help the neighborhood residents explore their options for coping with this problem. For instance, a class-action lawsuit could be brought against the companies that dumped the chemicals. If it could be proved that the companies are at fault (that is, that they acted knowingly or negligently), they could be held financially liable for their actions.

The mother of one child (Eric, 14) who has leukemia makes an appointment to see you. When she enters your office, she bursts into tears: "I am so angry! How could people do this to little children? They must have known that dumping those wastes so close to children was dangerous."

How do you respond empathically?

- "You sound really angry. I don't blame you. What are your thoughts about what to do?"
- "I'm hearing you say that you are furious about this situation. What can I do to help you?"
- "This whole situation has been a horror story for you. Where do you think we can go from here?"

Vignette #2: You are a social worker in a health care facility for older adults. You want to start a program that will bring middle-school children to visit your senior clients. You believe that such interactions will be mutually beneficial for both your clients and the children. You have approached Kimberly, the other social worker in the facility, with this idea, but her response was hesitant and—in your opinion—negative. You think she is worried that this proposal will create a lot more work for her, work that she is neither ready nor willing to undertake.

In fact, you have pretty much paved the way for implementing the plan.   You have contacted school administrators and teachers to obtain their permission and support. You've come up with a transportation plan and a proposed form for parental permissions. Before you have the chance to approach Kimberly again, she initiates a conversation with you. She states, "I know you're trying to do the right thing with this student visitation project [this is an empathic response on Kimberly's part], *but* you're pushing me into it. I don't have enough time to do my own work, let alone get involved in some petty little program you propose."

How do you respond empathically? (Remember that you *do not have to solve the problem right now*. You simply need to let Kimberly know that you understand how she feels.)

Alternative Response #1:

Alternative Response #2:

Vignette #3: You are a social worker at a diagnostic and treatment center for children with multiple physical disabilities. Your primary function is helping parents cope with the pressures they are under and connecting them with needed resources. The center's staff includes a wide range of disciplines such as occupational therapy,[1] physical therapy,[2] speech therapy, psychology, and nursing. Sometimes the professionals from these other disciplines ask you to talk parents out of asking them questions, especially when a child's condition is getting worse. One day a physical therapist approaches you and asks, "Do you think you could talk to Mrs. Harris? She keeps asking me these uncomfortable questions about Sally [Mrs. Harris's daughter]. Sally's condition is deteriorating. I don't know what to say."
How do you respond empathically?

Alternative Response #1:

Alternative Response #2:

Vignette #4: You are an intake worker at a social services agency in a rural area. Your job is to take telephone calls, assess problems, and refer clients to the most appropriate services. You identify a gap in the services available to people with developmental disabilities. You think that a social activities center would help to fill this gap by meeting some hitherto unmet needs. You talk with administrators in your agency, and they generally support the idea—but they don't know where the funding would come from. They suggest that you talk with some local politicians. You make an appointment with the President of the County Board to explain your idea and ask about possible funding. She responds, "It certainly sounds good, but who's going to pay for it and run it?"

---

[1] *Occupational therapy* is "therapy that utilizes useful and creative activities to facilitate psychological or physical rehabilitation" (Nichols, *Random House Webster's College Dictionary,* 1999, p. 914).

[2] *Physical therapy* is "the treatment or management of physical disability, malfunction, or pain by physical techniques, such as exercise, massage, hydrotherapy, etc." (Nichols, 1999, p. 887).

How do you respond empathetically?

Alternative Response #1:

Alternative Response #2:

Competencies/Practice Behaviors Exercise 2.2
Responding to Others in the Macro Environment

Focus Competencies or Practice Behaviors:
- EP 2.1.10b   Use empathy and other interpersonal skills

Instructions:
A.   Review the material below on communicating with people in macro contexts. Nine common verbal responses are briefly defined
B.   Read each of the statements in the second box. These might come from colleagues, supervisors, administrators, and others in the macro working environment
C.   For each statement, give examples of the different types of possible responses (the types are listed under each statement)
D.   **Statement # 1 provides an example**

USING VERBAL RESPONSES IN MACRO CONTEXTS

1.   **Simple Encouragement:** *Any verbal or nonverbal behavior intended to assure, comfort, or support the communication.*
2.   **Paraphrasing:** *Stating what the other person is saying, but using different words.*
3.   **Reflective Responding:** *Translating into words what you think the other person is feeling.*
4.   **Clarification:** *Choosing and using words to make certain that what another person has said is clearly understood.*
5.   **Interpretation:** *To seek meaning beyond that of clarification by helping bring a matter to a conclusion, to enlighten, or to seek a meaning of greater depth than that which has been stated.*
6.   **Providing Information:** *The communication of knowledge.*
7.   **Emphasizing People's Strengths:** *Articulating and emphasizing other people's positive characteristics and behaviors.*
8.   **Summarization:** *Covering the main points of a discussion or series of communications both briefly and concisely.*
9.   **Eliciting Information:** *Requesting knowledge you need.*

12

Statement #1: **(From a worker at another agency)** "I've been meaning to talk to you about your agency's policy regarding the treatment of poor clients."

Possible Responses:

Simple encouragement: "I see. Please go on."

Rephrasing: "You have some concerns about my agency's procedures for working with impoverished clients."

Reflective responding: "You're upset about the way my agency treats poor clients."

Clarification: "You're concerned about the effect of our sliding fee scale on clients who can't afford it."

Interpretation: "You have some ethical concerns about our policy on treatment of poor clients."

Providing information: "Let me give you a copy of our new policy and some data on how it affects clients."

Emphasizing people's strengths: "You always have been an exceptional advocate for the poor."

Summarization: (Since it is almost impossible to summarize one line, assume that there has been an ongoing discussion of this matter.) "Over the past few weeks, we've talked about a number of your concerns about agency policy, including treatment of staff, of people of color, and of the poor."

Eliciting information: "Can you tell me exactly which policy you are referring to?"

Statement #2: **(From a colleague at your agency)** "I'm furious with my supervisor. He never gives me credit for anything!"

Simple encouragement:

Rephrasing:

Reflective responding:

Clarification:

Interpretation:

Providing information:

Emphasizing people's strengths:

Summarization: (Since it is almost impossible to summarize one line, assume that you have had an ongoing discussion on this matter.)

Eliciting information:

Statement #3: **(From another agency's director)** "I think your agency ought to get more involved in our vocational rehabilitation program."[3]

Simple encouragement:

Rephrasing:

Reflective responding:

Clarification:

Interpretation:

Providing information:

Emphasizing people's strengths:

---

[3] *Vocational rehabilitation* involves training people who have physical or mental disabilities "so they can do useful work, become more self-sufficient, and be less reliant on public financial assistance" (Barker, 2003, p. 457).

Summarization: (Since it is almost impossible to summarize one line, assume that you have had an ongoing discussion on this matter.)

Eliciting information:

Statement #4: **(From a local politician who has significant influence over your agency's funding)** "I'd like to know why your agency's staff hasn't submitted any grants for external funding."

Simple encouragement:

Rephrasing:

Reflective responding:

Clarification:

Interpretation:

Providing information:

Emphasizing people's strengths:

Summarization: (Since it is almost impossible to summarize one line, assume that you have had an ongoing discussion on this matter.)

Eliciting information:

Competencies/Practice Behaviors Exercise 2.3
Nonassertive, Aggressive, and Assertive Responses

Focus Competencies or Practice Behaviors:
- EP 2.1.1b   Practice personal reflection and self-correction to assure continual professional development

Instructions:

A.   Review the material on appropriate assertiveness in the macro environment. Brief definitions are provided in the box below

B.   Read the scenarios and respond to the subsequent questions

---

Brief Definitions Regarding Assertiveness

Nonassertive communication: Meek verbal and nonverbal behavior coming from a speaker who devalues herself completely, feeling the other person and what that person thinks are much more important than her own thoughts.

Aggressive communication: Bold and dominating verbal and nonverbal behavior whereby a speaker presses her point of view as taking precedence above all other points of view, considering only her own views important, not the views of others.

Assertive communication: Verbal and nonverbal behavior that permits a speaker to get her points across clearly and straightforwardly, taking into consideration both her own value and the values of whomever is receiving her message.

Scenario A: You are a social worker for Heterogeneous County Department of Social Services. Paperwork recording your activities with clients is due promptly the Monday following the last day of each month. For whatever reason, you simply forget to get it in by 5:00 p.m. Monday the day it's due. Your supervisor Enrique calls you at noon the next day. He raises his voice and reprimands, "You know that reports are due promptly so that funding is not jeopardized. How many times do I have to tell you that?"

Nonassertive Response:

Aggressive Response:

Assertive Response:

Costs and benefits of each type of response:

Scenario B: You work with a colleague who consistently comes late to your social work unit's biweekly meetings. He typically saunters leisurely into the meeting room with a cup of decaf in hand, noisily situates himself in a chair at the rectangular meeting table, and casually interrupts whomever is speaking, asking for a brief review of what he missed. You are sick and tired of such rude, time-wasting behavior.

Nonassertive Response:

Aggressive Response:

Assertive Response:

Costs and benefits of each type of response:

Scenario C: You represent your social services agency at a community meeting where twelve community residents and five workers from other agencies are discussing what additional social services the community needs. Some possible grant funding has become available to develop services. The person chairing the meeting asks for input from each person present except you. Apparently, she simply overlooked that you had not gotten an opportunity to speak.

Nonassertive Response:

Aggressive Response:

17

Assertive Response:

Costs and benefits of each type of response:

- *Nonassertive Response:*

Aggressive Response:

Assertive Response:

Costs and benefits of each type of response:

Nonassertive Response:

18

Aggressive Response:

Assertive Response:

Costs and benefits of each type of response:

Scenario F: Hiroko is a public assistance worker for a large county bureaucracy. She is very dedicated to her job and often spends extra time with clients to make certain that they receive all possible benefits. Her colleague Bill, who has the same job title, tells Hiroko, "Either you're a fool and a drudge to work overtime like that, or you're trying to be a 'star' to feed your ego."

Nonassertive Response:

Aggressive Response:

Assertive Response:

Costs and benefits of each type of response:

Competencies/Practice Behaviors Exercise 2. 4
Assertiveness Training for You

Focus Competencies or Practice Behaviors:
- EP 2.1.1b   Practice personal reflection and self-correction to assure continual professional development

Instructions:
A.   Review the material on assertiveness and assertiveness training
B.   Recall a situation in which you could have acted more assertively. Perhaps you were too nonassertive or too aggressive. Describe the situation below

C.   Analyze the way you reacted in this situation. Critically examine both your verbal and nonverbal behavior. Describe and explain that behavior

D.   Choose a role model for assertive behavior in a situation similar to the one you have described. Identify the person you've chosen, then describe what happened and how she reacted assertively

E.   Identify two or three other assertive verbal and nonverbal responses that you could have employed in the situation you described

F.   Imagine yourself acting assertively in the situation you described. Explain what you would say and do

G.   After you have completed these five steps, try behaving assertively in real life. Continue practicing until assertiveness becomes part of your personal interactive style. Give yourself a pat on the back when you succeed in becoming more assertive. Be patient with yourself—it's not easy to change long-standing patterns of behavior

Add more pages if necessary

Competencies/Practice Behaviors Exercise 2. 5
What's Your Style of Conflict?

Focus Competencies or Practice Behaviors:
- EP 2.1.1b   Practice personal reflection and self-correction to assure continual professional development

Instructions:
A.   Review the material on conflict and its resolution and the content on the use of "Why?"
B.   Read the material on the five styles of addressing conflict presented in the box below
C.   Answer the questions below concerning your own individual styles for handling conflict

---

Personal Styles for Addressing Conflict

Johnson (2009, p. 253) proposed the following five styles of addressing conflict:
1.   *Turtles* withdraw into their shells to avoid conflicts. For them, this is easier than mustering up the initiative and energy needed to address a conflict. Turtles typically have relatively poor self-concepts and are nonassertive.
2.   *Sharks,* unlike turtles, are aggressors. They move into conflict boldly, pushing aside any opponents. Sharks like power and want to win. They have very little interest in nurturing a relationship with an opponent.
3.   *Teddy bears* are essentially the opposite of sharks. They value their relationships with their opponent more than the achievement of their own goals. Teddy bears are more assertive than turtles because they do value their own ideas, but they will put those ideas aside in deference to an opponent's beliefs if they believe their relationship is threatened.
4.   *Foxes* are compromisers. Slyly, they work toward an agreement acceptable to them and to their opponent. Foxes are willing to relinquish some of their demands in order to come to a reasonable compromise. They are pretty slick at finding ways to satisfy everyone.

---

1.   What style of conflict—or combination of styles—described above comes closest to the way you usually handle a conflict?

2.   To what extent is your approach to handling conflict effective? Explain.

3. 　　　In what ways would you like to change your approach to conflict management? (If you are satisfied with your behavior in conflict situations, say so.)

Competencies/Practice Behaviors Exercise 2. 6
Conflict Resolution

Focus Competencies or Practice Behaviors:
- EP 2.1.3c 　　Demonstrate effective oral and written communication in working with individuals, families, groups, organizations, communities, and colleagues
- EP 2.1.10g 　Select appropriate intervention strategies

Instructions:
A. 　　　Review the material on confrontation and conflict resolution. A *confrontation* is a face-to-face encounter where people come together with opposing opinions, perspectives, or ideas in order to scrutinize or compare them. See the material summarized in the box below on conflict resolution

> ***Steps in Conflict Resolution***
>
> The following seven steps of conflict resolution are proposed (Ivey & Ivey, 2008; Ivey et al., 2010; Johnson, 2009):
>
> ***Step 1:*** *The confrontation.* First, clearly identify and examine your personal goals. Second, keep in mind that it's important to nurture your relationship with your opponent.
>
> ***Step 2:*** *Establish common ground.* This definition should make neither you nor your opponent defensive or resistant to compromise. Emphasize how important the issue is to both of you.
>
> ***Step 3:*** *Emphasize the importance of communication.* Use the good communication techniques you have learned including the following (Sheafor and Horejsi (2009, pp. 382-383):
> 　　a. Do not begin a confrontation when you're angry.
> 　　b. Do not enter into a conflict unless you have a clearly established reason for doing so.
> 　　c. If you absolutely despise your opponent or have immense difficulty reaching for any positive, empathic feelings about him, do not confront him.
> 　　d. Include positive statements and feedback along with the negative aspects of confrontation.
> 　　e. Be certain to explain your concerns regarding the conflict in a "descriptive and nonjudgmental" manner (Sheafor & Horejsi, 2009, p. 383).
> 　　f. Supply relevant data in support of your stance.
> 　　g. An additional suggestion is to use 'I-messages' frequently.
>
> ***Step 4:*** *Emphasize your own willingness to cooperate.* To minimize disagreement (or at least to develop a viable plan of action) stress whatever you and your opponent have in common.

22

Step 5: *Empathize with your opponent's perspective.* Think carefully about why she thinks, feels, or acts as she does.

Step 6: *Evaluate both your own and your opponent's motivation to address the conflict.* Is it worthwhile to expend the energy necessary to resolve this conflict?

Step 7: Come to some mutually satisfactory agreement by following these five suggestions (Johnson, 2009):
   a. Articulate exactly what your agreement entails.
   b. Indicate how you will behave toward the other person in the future as compared to in the past.
   c. Specify how the other person will behave toward you.
   d. Agree on ways to address any future mistakes (that is, if you or the other behaves differently than you have agreed to
   e. Establish how and when you and the other person will meet in the future to continue your cooperative behavior and minimization conflict.

B.   Recall a conflict in which you have been involved. For the purposes of this exercise, it may be work-related, school-related, or personal. Answer the following questions

   1.   Describe the conflict in detail. Who was involved? What was the issue? Explain the positions taken by the opposing sides. What were the circumstances of the actual confrontation?

   2.   Did you follow the suggestions in Step 1 for beginning a confrontation—that is, did you identify your goals and nurture your relationship with your opponent? What, if anything, could you have done differently to improve your handling of this conflict?

   3.   Did you follow Step 2 by finding some common ground with your opponent? What, if anything, could you have done differently to discover some common ground?

   4.   Did you follow Step 3 by maintaining communication with your opponent? What, if anything, could you have done differently to improve communication?

5. Did you follow Step 4 by indicating your willingness to cooperate with your opponent? What, if anything, could you have done differently to demonstrate this willingness?

6. Did you follow Step 5 by empathizing with your opponent and trying to understand his or her perspective? What, if anything, could you have done differently to achieve this empathy and understanding?

7. Did you follow Step 6 by evaluating both your own and your opponent's motivations in this conflict? What, if anything, could you have done differently to discern and evaluate those motives?

8. Did you follow Step 7 by arriving at some mutually satisfactory agreement? What, if anything, could you have done differently to make such an agreement possible?

Competencies/Practice Behaviors Exercise 2. 7
Using Communication Techniques with Supervisors

Focus Competencies or Practice Behaviors:
- EP 2.1.3c   Demonstrate effective oral and written communication in working with individuals, families, groups, organizations, communities, and colleagues

Instructions:
A.   Review the material on communicating with other people in macro contexts and working under supervisors. Communication techniques are summarized in the box below
B.   For each of the following statements made by supervisors to their supervisees, give examples of the different types of possible statements you might make or questions you might ask as a supervisee making a response
C.   Label which verbal response or combination of responses indicated in the box above each statement reflects. Formulate as many types of the nine verbal responses as possible
D.   Because the statements are vague, feel free to make up facts in your responses

24

USING VERBAL RESPONSES IN MACRO CONTEXTS

1. **Simple Encouragement:** *Any verbal or nonverbal behavior intended to assure, comfort, or support the communication.*
2. **Paraphrasing:** *Stating what the other person is saying, but using different words.*
3. **Reflective Responding:** *Translating into words what you think the other person is feeling.*
4. **Clarification:** *Choosing and using words to make certain that what another person has said is clearly understood.*
5. **Interpretation:** *To seek meaning beyond that of clarification by helping bring a matter to a conclusion, to enlighten, or to seek a meaning of greater depth than that which has been stated.*
6. **Providing Information:** *The communication of knowledge.*
7. **Emphasizing People's Strengths:** *Articulating and emphasizing other people's positive characteristics and behaviors.*
8. **Summarization:** *Covering the main points of a discussion or series of communications both briefly and concisely.*
9. **Eliciting Information:** *Requesting knowledge you need.*

Supervisor Statement A: I'm concerned about the quality of your work lately. It seems you've taken a lot of sick days and your record keeping has fallen behind.

As a supervisee, how might you respond?

What type(s) of verbal response or responses does this reflect? Explain why. (For example: "You sound like you're frustrated with me.") *Reflective responding*

"What work are you most concerned about?" *Eliciting information*

Supervisor Statement B: "There's an important staff meeting scheduled after work on Friday. I wouldn't make you attend if I didn't have to."

As a supervisee, how might you respond?

What type(s) of verbal response or responses does this reflect? Explain why.

Supervisor Statement C: "Could you work up a one-hour in-service training program[1] on some aspect of your practice for the general agency staff meeting next month?"

As a supervisee, how might you respond?

What type(s) of verbal response or responses does this reflect?

Supervisor Statement D: "Funding has been drastically cut. I surely wish someone around here knew more about grant writing."

As a supervisee, how might you respond?

What type(s) of verbal response or responses does this reflect?

---

[1] *In-service training programs* are educational sessions provided by an agency for its staff to develop their skills or improve their effectiveness.

26

As a supervisee, how might you respond?

What type(s) of verbal response or responses does this reflect?

Competencies/Practice Behaviors Exercise 2. 8
Addressing Problems in Supervision

Focus Competencies or Practice Behaviors:
- EP 2.1.1f   Use supervision and consultation

Instructions:
A.   Review the material on supervision
B.   Sometimes, for whatever reason, problems develop with supervisors. They may be your own, your supervisor's, or no one's fault, but when they occur, you must address them, adjust to them, or leave for another job
C.   The following scenarios are taken from actual supervisory experiences. Each involves real problems that you too could confront. In each case, think about how you might address the problem. Then answer the questions that follow

Scenario A: Taking Your Credit
     You are a social worker at a large urban diagnostic and treatment center for children with multiple developmental and physical disabilities. Your primary role includes helping parents cope with their child's disability, making referrals to appropriate resources, offering some family counseling, and interpreting the physicians' and other therapists' findings and recommendations to parents in words the parents can understand.
     The city abruptly cuts off funding for transportation to the center. Many of your parents are very poor and don't own vehicles. Most of the children have such extreme physical difficulties that city buses can't accommodate them. After compiling some facts, you call various local political leaders and share with them your serious concerns. Because of your efforts, the local City Council Chairperson convenes a meeting to address and remedy this transportation problem. You are very proud of yourself because you feel you are primarily responsible for this solution.
     You share the news with your supervisor and indicate enthusiastically that you are planning to attend the meeting. She says, "I don't think you need to attend the meeting. I'll go instead." You emphasize how hard you've worked on this project and make clear that you would really like to attend. You suggest that, perhaps, you could both go.
     She responds, "No, I don't think so. I'll go." You are devastated.

1. Try to empathize with this supervisor by discerning what her reasons might be for reacting like this.

2. In this situation, how could you use the suggestions for assertiveness and confrontation described earlier in this chapter?

3. Consider the suggestions for using supervision effectively. Which of them could help you in this case?

4. If you were the supervisee portrayed here, how important would it be to you to receive credit for your accomplishment? Would you feel that it was the goal that mattered rather than *who* achieved it?

5. If you are the supervisee portrayed here and you *do* care about receiving credit for your work, what will you do if all the suggestions you have proposed thus far fail? (For example, will you go to an administrator above your supervisor for help and risk your supervisor's wrath? Will you learn a lesson from the experience and keep your successes to yourself in the future? Will you try to put it out of your mind and go on with your daily business? Will you start looking for another job?) There is no "correct" answer. You must identify various options, weigh the pros and cons of each, and decide what to do.

Scenario B: The Communication Gap

You are a newly hired social worker for a unit of boys, ages 11 to 13, at a residential treatment center for youths with serious behavioral and emotional problems. Your responsibilities include counseling, group work, case management, some family counseling, and consultation with child-care staff on matters of behavioral programming. Two of the twelve boys in the unit have been causing you particular trouble. They are late for their weekly counseling sessions and sometimes skip them altogether. When you do talk to them, they don't respond to your questions. Instead, they walk around the room, tell you that you don't know what you're doing, poke holes in the furniture with their pencils, and call you vulgar names.

You are at a loss regarding what to do with these two clients. In your weekly one-hour session with your supervisor, you explain the situation. He makes several vague suggestions about videotaping some of your sessions, making home visits, and talking about the boys' behavior with them. At the end of the session, you feel you've gotten nowhere, and you still don't understand what you should do. You have difficulty following what your supervisor is saying. You can't "read" him. Sometimes you think he's joking, but you can't be sure.

1.   Try to empathize with this supervisor by discerning what his reasons might be for reacting like this.

2.   In this situation, how could you use the suggestions for assertiveness and confrontation described earlier in this chapter?

3.   Consider the suggestions for using supervision effectively. Which of them could help you in this case?

4.   Consider the possibility that you tried a range of approaches and none worked. If you decided that your supervisor was incompetent and really unable to help you, what would you do?   Might you consider turning to other people in the agency for help? If so, how would you do so?

Scenario C: The Angry Response

You are a social worker at a health care center (nursing home) who has a variety of clients diagnosed as "mentally ill." Every six months, a staffing is held at which social workers, nurses, therapists (speech, occupational, physical), physicians, psychologists, and psychiatrists summarize clients' progress and make recommendations.   It is your job to run the staffing and write a summary of what is said.

You are new at your job and unfamiliar with this agency. During the staffing, the psychiatrist is very verbal—in fact, you would describe him as "pushy." You feel intimidated and are uncomfortable asserting your own opinions when they are different from, or even opposed to, his. Because of his advanced education, his professional status, and his self-confident demeanor, you feel that his views are probably more important and valid than yours. After the staffing, your supervisor calls you aside. His face is red and his voice has a deadly, steel-like calm. He reams you out for letting the psychiatrist take over the staffing. This surprises and upsets you so much that you do not hear many of the specific things he says. You just know that he is furious with you and has implied—or even stated—that you are an incompetent wimp. He walks off in a huff.

1.   Try to empathize with this supervisor by discerning what his reasons might be for reacting like this.

2.   In this situation, how could you use the suggestions for assertiveness and confrontation described earlier in this chapter?

3.   Consider the suggestions for using supervision effectively. Which of them could help you in this case?

Scenario D: Problems with Delegation[5]

You are a caseworker for a social services agency in a rural county. Your job includes a wide range of social work practice, from investigating child abuse cases to working with families of truants to providing supplementary services to older adults who want to remain in their own homes. You have a heavy caseload, but feel very useful. In general, you really like your job.

The problem is that your supervisor insists on reading every letter and report you write before it goes out. You think this is a terribly time-consuming waste of effort. In many instances, it also delays your provision of service, and you feel that it's condescending and implies a lack of confidence in your professional abilities.

1.   Try to empathize with this supervisor by discerning what her reasons might be for reacting like this.

2.   In this situation, how could you use the suggestions for assertiveness and confrontation described earlier in this chapter?

3.   Consider the suggestions for using supervision effectively. Which of them could help you in this case?

---

[5] A primary administrative task for supervisors is mastering the art of delegation. *Delegation* is "assigning responsibility or authority to others" (Mish, *Webster's Ninth New Collegiate Dictionary*, 1991, p. 336).

4.	In the event that your efforts to improve this situation fail, what would you do?

Scenario E: No Action

You are a social worker in a large urban community center serving multiple community needs. Services include counseling for emotional and behavior problems, provision of contraception, recreational activities for adults and youth, day care for working parents, meals for older adult citizens, some health care, and a variety of other services. Your job focuses primarily on counseling the center's clients referred for this purpose. You enjoy your job and are proud of being a professional social worker.

The problem is another social worker whose office is next to yours. He has a similar job but is assigned a different caseload and a slightly different range of responsibilities. The bottom line is that you seriously question his professional competence. You've observed him using what you'd describe as "comic book therapy" with the children and adolescents on his caseload. In other words, his clients come in and select comic books from his vast collection instead of receiving any real counseling. He has boasted on several occasions that he only went into social work because he was eligible for a scholarship.

One day you approach one of your clients, a fairly bright and articulate boy of 13. You are surprised to see him reading something in the center's waiting room, and you are disturbed when he obtrusively places his hand over a portion of a picture in the book. It strikes you as odd that his hand is placed over the rear half of a horse. He looks surprised to see you and he comments on the horse's long white mane. The mane is indeed remarkable: it reaches to the ground and extends another foot. When you ask your client what the book is about, he sheepishly shows you the picture, which depicts a castrated horse (hence, the mane and tail elongated due to hormonal changes). The book's title is *Washington Death Trips*. Among other items pictured in the book are dead babies in caskets, people who have butchered over 500 chickens by hand for no reason, and various infamous murderers. The boy tells you that your colleague lent him this book.

You are furious. Not only does this colleague offend your professionalism and your professional ethics, he even has the gall to interfere with your clients. You immediately go to your supervisor, who is also his supervisor, and complain about the incident.

Your supervisor—a well-liked, easy-going, but knowledgeable and helpful person—hems and haws. He implies that methods of counseling are each professional's own business, but you believe that your supervisor is afraid to confront your colleague.

1.	Try to empathize with this supervisor by discerning what his reasons might be for reacting like this.

32

2.   In this situation, how could you use the suggestions for assertiveness and confrontation described earlier in this chapter?

3.   Consider the suggestions for using supervision effectively. Which of them could help you in this case?

4.   If your efforts to improve this situation fail, what will you do? Can you ignore this issue?

Competencies/Practice Behaviors Exercise 2. 9
A Role Play in Supervision

Focus Competencies or Practice Behaviors:
- EP 2.1.1f   Use supervision and consultation

Instructions:
A.   Review the material on assertiveness in the macro environment, and conflict resolution, supervision, and worker's general expectations of supervisors. A summary of worker's general expectations of supervisors is presented in the box below
B.   For this exercise you should pair off with another classmate, with one person playing a supervisee and the other a supervisor. You and your partner choose who will play which role. The supervisee should use the suggestions provided in this chapter to confront the supervisor assertively and use supervision effectively. After five to ten minutes, stop and answer the questions

> ***Supervisee:*** *You are a generalist practitioner in a foster care placement unit in a large county social services agency. You received your annual performance review report from your supervisor. The format requires a summary statement by the supervisor. Yours reads, "This worker does a pretty good job of completing her work on time." You feel this is a very negative statement, substantially detracting from a positive evaluation. You believe that you work exceptionally hard, often volunteer to accept difficult cases, and take pride in your performance.*
>
> ***Supervisor:*** *You have two dozen supervisees. You don't like to give radically different performance reviews to your workers because these can make for hard feelings and jealousy among staff. You don't think the review is really relevant anyway since salaries are based solely on seniority, not on merit. In your view, your significant communication with workers is carried on during your biweekly individual supervisory conferences, and you think this particular supervisee is doing a good job.*

1.　　What communication, confrontation, assertiveness, and supervisory techniques did the supervisee use during the role play?

2.　　How effective were these techniques in resolving the issue?

3.　　What other techniques, if any, might the supervisee have used to improve her effectiveness?

Chapter 2 Competencies or Practice Behaviors Exercises Assessment:

Name: _____ **Date:** _____

Supervisor's Name: _____

Focus Competencies/Practice Behaviors:
- EP 2.1.1b   Practice personal reflection and self-correction to assure continual professional development
- EP 2.1.1f   Use supervision and consultation
- EP 2.1.3c   Demonstrate effective oral and written communication in working with individuals, families, groups, organizations, communities, and colleagues
- EP 2.1.10b   Use empathy and other interpersonal skills
- EP 2.1.10g   Select appropriate intervention strategies

Instructions:

A.   Evaluate your work or your partner's work in the Focus Competencies/Practice Behaviors by completing the Competencies/Practice Behaviors Assessment form below

B.   What other Competencies/Practice Behaviors did you use to complete these Exercises? Be sure to record them in your assessments

1.	I have attained this competency/practice behavior (in the range of 81 to 100%)
2.	I have largely attained this competency/practice behavior (in the range of 61 to 80%)
3.	I have partially attained this competency/practice behavior (in the range of 41 to 60%)
4.	I have made a little progress in attaining this competency/practice behavior (in the range of 21 to 40%)
5.	I have made almost no progress in attaining this competency/practice behavior (in the range of 0 to 20%)

EPAS 2008 Core Competencies & Core Practice Behaviors		Student Self Assessment						Evaluator Feedback
Student and Evaluator Assessment Scale and Comments		0	1	2	3	4	5	Agree/Disagree/Comments
EP 2.1.1 Identify as a Professional Social Worker and Conduct Oneself Accordingly								
a.	Advocate for client access to the services of social work							
b.	Practice personal reflection and self-correction to assure continual professional development							
c.	Attend to professional roles and boundaries							
d.	Demonstrate professional demeanor in behavior, appearance, and communication							
e.	Engage in career-long learning							
f.	Use supervision and consultation							
EP 2.1.2 Apply Social Work Ethical Principles to Guide Professional Practice								
a.	Recognize and manage personal values in a way that allows professional values to guide practice							
b.	Make ethical decisions by applying NASW Code of Ethics and, as applicable, of the IFSW/IASSW Ethics in Social Work, Statement of Principles							
c.	Tolerate ambiguity in resolving ethical conflicts							
d.	Apply strategies of ethical reasoning to arrive at principled decisions							

EP 2.1.3 Apply Critical Thinking to Inform and Communicate Professional Judgments							
a. Distinguish, appraise, and integrate multiple sources of knowledge, including research-based knowledge and practice wisdom							
b. Analyze models of assessment, prevention, intervention, and evaluation							
c. Demonstrate effective oral and written communication in working with individuals, families, groups, organizations, communities, and colleagues							
EP 2.1.4 Engage Diversity and Difference in Practice							
a. Recognize the extent to which a culture's structures and values may oppress, marginalize, alienate, or create or enhance privilege and power							
b. Gain sufficient self-awareness to eliminate the influence of personal biases and values in working with diverse groups							
c. Recognize and communicate their understanding of the importance of difference in shaping life experiences							
d. View themselves as learners and engage those with whom they work as informants							
EP 2.1.5 Advance Human Rights and Social and Economic Justice							
a. Understand forms and mechanisms of oppression and discrimination							
b. Advocate for human rights and social and economic justice							
c. Engage in practices that advance social and economic justice							
EP 2.1.6 Engage in Research-Informed Practice and Practice-Informed Research							
a. Use practice experience to inform scientific inquiry							
b. Use research evidence to inform practice							
EP 2.1.7 Apply Knowledge of Human Behavior and the Social Environment							
a. Utilize conceptual frameworks to guide the processes of assessment, intervention, and evaluation							
b. Critique and apply knowledge to understand person and environment							
EP 2.1.8 Engage in Policy Practice to Advance Social and Economic Well-Being and to Deliver Effective Social Work Services							
a. Analyze, formulate, and advocate for policies that advance social well-being							
b. Collaborate with colleagues and clients for effective policy action							
EP 2.1.9 Respond to Contexts that Shape Practice							
a. Continuously discover, appraise, and attend to changing locales, populations, scientific and technological developments, and emerging societal trends to provide relevant services							
b. Provide leadership in promoting sustainable changes in service delivery and practice to improve the quality of social services							

EP 2.1.10 Engage, Assess, Intervene, and Evaluate with Individuals, Families, Groups, Organizations and Communities							
a.	Substantively and affectively prepare for action with individuals, families, groups, organizations, and communities						
b.	Use empathy and other interpersonal skills						
c.	Develop a mutually agreed-on focus of work and desired outcomes						
d.	Collect, organize, and interpret client data						
e.	Assess client strengths and limitations						
f.	Develop mutually agreed-on intervention goals and objectives						
g.	Select appropriate intervention strategies						
h.	Initiate actions to achieve organizational goals						
i.	Implement prevention interventions that enhance client capacities						
j.	Help clients resolve problems						
k.	Negotiate, mediate, and advocate for clients						
l.	Facilitate transitions and endings						
m.	Critically analyze, monitor, and evaluate interventions						

Chapter 3
Group Skills for Organizational and Community Change

Competencies/Practice Behaviors Exercise 3.1
Identifying Your Own Networks

Focus Competencies or Practice Behaviors:
- EP 2.1.1b Practice personal reflection and self-correction to assure continual professional development

Instructions:
A.   In the table below, identify the networks of which you are a part
B.   Differentiate which are professional and which are personal by placing a checkmark under the appropriate category

Network	Professional	Personal	Situation Number

C.   Read the situations in the box below. Which of your networks would be helpful in any of these situations? Place the situation number in the appropriate places on the table above

---

Which of Your Networks Might be Helpful in These Situations?

1.   You need advice about a personal problem.
2.   You want to know how to register to vote in your community.
3.   You need to refer a client to a substance abuse program.
4.   You need to help a client getting a temporary restraining order.
5.   Your car breaks down on the way to your first day at your field placement. You need a ride to work for the next two days.
6.   Payday is still a week away and you need another $50 to get a wart removed from your nose.
7.   Your computer and printer just quit, you have a paper due tomorrow morning at 8:00 a.m., and the campus computer labs are closed.
8.   You have decided to come out of the closet and acknowledge that you are gay (or lesbian). Who is the first person you could depend on for support?

Competencies/Practice Behaviors Exercise 3.2
Teamwork

Focus Competencies or Practice Behaviors:
- EP 2.1.1b Practice personal reflection and self-correction to assure continual professional development
- EP 2.1.10 Engage, assess, intervene, and evaluate with individuals, families, groups, organizations, and communities

Instructions:
A. List three groups or teams of which you are a member. These can be from your work, class, or personal life
B. Using the characteristics of effective teams noted in the box below, identify which (if any) of these groups/teams were particularly effective

Characteristics of Effective Teams
1. Clear goals
2. Structure and membership tied to goals
3. Commitment of members (team spirit)
4. A climate of collaboration
5. Commitment to excellence
6. External recognition and support
7. Principled leadership

Group or Team	Reasons Why It Was Effective or Ineffective
1.	
2.	
3.	

Competencies/Practice Behaviors Exercise 3.3
Conflict

Focus Competencies or Practice Behaviors:
- EP 2.1.1b Practice personal reflection and self-correction to assure continual professional development
- EP 2.1.3c Demonstrate effective oral and written communication in working with individuals, families, groups, organizations, communities, and colleagues

Instructions:
A. Identify two conflicts in which you have been involved in your school, work, or personal life and write them in the following table
B. Indicate whether each conflict was an interpersonal, resource, representational, or intercessional conflict

39

C.   Explain why you chose each particular type of conflict

Identify Conflict	Category	Reasons for Choosing This Category
1.		
2.		

Competencies/Practice Behaviors Exercise 3.4
Recognizing Types of Conflict

Focus Competencies or Practice Behaviors:
- EP 2.1.3   Apply critical thinking to inform and communicate professional judgments

Instructions:
A.   Read each of the snippets below and identify the type of conflict you believe is being displayed
B.   Provide a brief explanation for your choice

Conflict Snippets

1.   "As chair of the homeless coalition, I can't sit here and let this city council tear down the old courthouse without a fight. We have 50 homeless families in this city and the city owns a building that would make a wonderful shelter. Mayor Jones, why can't you see the benefits that using this structure for a shelter would bring to the community?"

"The city council has to be concerned about more than just homeless people, Ed. We need the space occupied by the old courthouse for downtown parking. We're losing business to the mall outside of town because we have no place for people to park downtown. The city council asked me to work with you to find some other solution for this homeless problem."

Type of Conflict:

Explain:

2.   "If we add money to the budget so we can hire another building inspector, we won't be able to put another police officer on the force. What with the increase in gang activity here, I believe we need more cops, not more building inspectors."

"Figuring out what makes the most sense within the budget is important, Mary. We have only $75,000 left in the personnel budget. I think the money will produce better benefits for the community if we add the inspector. There are too many substandard homes and apartments in the community, some of which are being used as drug houses. An inspector could help us cope with this at least as well as another police officer."

Type of Conflict:

Explain:

---

3.   "Constanza, I am tired of hearing of the so-called benefits of the DARE program. Show me an ounce of research that proves this program actually keeps school kids from using drugs. The whole thing is just a big public relations program. I think we should concentrate our efforts on something we know works—like the Police Dog Sniffer program. We know the dogs can sniff out drugs in school lockers."

"José, police dogs are fine after the fact, but they do nothing to prevent drug use. We should spend our money on prevention, not intervention."

Type of Conflict:

Explain:

---

4.   "You're on their side! Why don't you ever see our perspective? All you ever do is agree with the Razers."

"Oh, right. Man, if he's on our side we're in big trouble. He can't understand anything 'cause he's not a home boy."

"Washington, Alonzo, I'm not on anyone's side. I'm supposed to find a way to keep you from stomping each other and keep you out of jail besides. My point is that I think the Guns' proposal to keep the downtown area off limits to gang activity makes sense. It lets both your groups use the downtown as individuals, and it keeps the police off your butts. The minute you start something downtown, you've got the mayor, the council, and business owners turning up the heat. Both of your gangs get fried whenever that happens. Just because Alonzo suggested it, doesn't make it automatically a bad idea. Now get out of my face unless you have a better idea."

Type of Conflict:

Explain:

Focus Competencies or Practice Behaviors:
- EP 2.1.3   Apply critical thinking to inform and communicate professional judgments
- EP 2.1.5b   Advocate for human rights and social and economic justice
- EP 2.1.8b   Collaborate with colleagues and clients for effective policy action
- EP 2.1.10k   Negotiate, mediate, and advocate for clients

Instructions:

A.   This role play will involve 5 people, each with his or her own idea of conflict management

B.   Assign each person to the role of Dwight, Miguel, Betty, Mel, and Teresa

C.   The meeting has been called to discuss a proposed hospital policy and has begun with the following conversation

D.   Continue with this role play for fifteen minutes and try to resolve this conflict

---

Scenario: A conflict is brewing within the staff of the Loving Arms Hospital social work department regarding how to handle a hospital-proposed reduction in patient services.

Dwight is a new worker in this unit and he is concerned about the apparent split developing over this proposal. He remembers the steps in managing conflict that he studied in his social work practice class. He writes them down so he can review them during the meetings.

Miguel, the most senior social worker in the unit, is speaking angrily about the situation: "We have always been a department that offered help to anyone we felt was at high risk. That risk could be financial, emotional, social, or medical. We've never set some group aside and said, 'We won't help you.' That's not what social work is all about."

"Micky, I know you're upset. But we don't own the hospital—we just work here. If the hospital director says we have to focus our services rather than take all comers, I don't see what we can do," says Betty, the acting department director.

 "You can't fight city hall," says Mel, another worker.

"Baloney," Teresa chimes in. "This hospital has built a fine reputation and we're not going to let it get destroyed without a fight."

---

1.   Circle which of the following types of conflict were displayed in the role play:
   a.   Interest-commitment
   b.   Induced
   c.   Misattributed
   d.   Data
   e.   Structural
   f.   Illusionary
   g.   Displaced
   h.   Expressive

2.   Who was displaying each type? How were these conflicts resolved?

_____

_____

_____

_____

_____

_____

_____

_____

3.   What conflict management strategies were used in this role play?

_____

_____

_____

_____

4.   With what conflict management strategy do you feel most comfortable? Why?

_____

_____

_____

_____

_____

Chapter 3 Competencies/Practice Behaviors Exercises Assessment:

Name: _____ **Date:** _____

Supervisor's Name: _____

Focus Competencies/Practice Behaviors:
- EP 2.1.1b Practice personal reflection and self-correction to assure continual professional development
- EP 2.1.3 Apply critical thinking to inform and communicate professional judgments
- EP 2.1.3c Demonstrate effective oral and written communication in working with individuals, families, groups, organizations, communities, and colleagues
- EP 2.1.5b Advocate for human rights and social and economic justice
- EP 2.1.8b Collaborate with colleagues and clients for effective policy action
- EP 2.1.10 Engage, assess, intervene, and evaluate with individuals, families, groups, organizations, and communities
- EP 2.1.10k Negotiate, mediate, and advocate for clients

Instructions:
A. Evaluate your work or your partner's work in the Focus Competencies/Practice Behaviors by completing the Competencies/Practice Behaviors Assessment form below
B. What other Competencies/Practice Behaviors did you use to complete these Exercises? Be sure to record them in your assessments

1.	I have attained this competency/practice behavior (in the range of 81 to 100%)
2.	I have largely attained this competency/practice behavior (in the range of 61 to 80%)
3.	I have partially attained this competency/practice behavior (in the range of 41 to 60%)
4.	I have made a little progress in attaining this competency/practice behavior (in the range of 21 to 40%)
5.	I have made almost no progress in attaining this competency/practice behavior (in the range of 0 to 20%)

Student and Evaluator Assessment Scale and Comments	0	1	2	3	4	5	Agree/Disagree/Comments
EP 2.1.1 Identify as a Professional Social Worker and Conduct Oneself Accordingly							
a. Advocate for client access to the services of social work							
b. Practice personal reflection and self-correction to assure continual professional development							
c. Attend to professional roles and boundaries							
d. Demonstrate professional demeanor in behavior, appearance, and communication							
e. Engage in career-long learning							
f. Use supervision and consultation							
EP 2.1.2 Apply Social Work Ethical Principles to Guide Professional Practice							
a. Recognize and manage personal values in a way that allows professional values to guide practice							
b. Make ethical decisions by applying NASW Code of Ethics and, as applicable, of the IFSW/IASSW Ethics in Social Work, Statement of Principles							
c. Tolerate ambiguity in resolving ethical conflicts							
d. Apply strategies of ethical reasoning to arrive at principled decisions							

44

EP 2.1.3 Apply Critical Thinking to Inform and Communicate Professional Judgments							
a.	Distinguish, appraise, and integrate multiple sources of knowledge, including research-based knowledge and practice wisdom						
b.	Analyze models of assessment, prevention, intervention, and evaluation						
c.	Demonstrate effective oral and written communication in working with individuals, families, groups, organizations, communities, and colleagues						
EP 2.1.4 Engage Diversity and Difference in Practice							
a.	Recognize the extent to which a culture's structures and values may oppress, marginalize, alienate, or create or enhance privilege and power						
b.	Gain sufficient self-awareness to eliminate the influence of personal biases and values in working with diverse groups						
c.	Recognize and communicate their understanding of the importance of difference in shaping life experiences						
d.	View themselves as learners and engage those with whom they work as informants						
EP 2.1.5 Advance Human Rights and Social and Economic Justice							
a.	Understand forms and mechanisms of oppression and discrimination						
b.	Advocate for human rights and social and economic justice						
c.	Engage in practices that advance social and economic justice						
EP 2.1.6 Engage in Research-Informed Practice and Practice-Informed Research							
a.	Use practice experience to inform scientific inquiry						
b.	Use research evidence to inform practice						
EP 2.1.7 Apply Knowledge of Human Behavior and the Social Environment							
a.	Utilize conceptual frameworks to guide the processes of assessment, intervention, and evaluation						
b.	Critique and apply knowledge to understand person and environment						
EP 2.1.8 Engage in Policy Practice to Advance Social and Economic Well-Being and to Deliver Effective Social Work Services							
a.	Analyze, formulate, and advocate for policies that advance social well-being						
b.	Collaborate with colleagues and clients for effective policy action						
EP 2.1.9 Respond to Contexts that Shape Practice							
a.	Continuously discover, appraise, and attend to changing locales, populations, scientific and technological developments, and emerging societal trends to provide relevant services						

b.	Provide leadership in promoting sustainable changes in service delivery and practice to improve the quality of social services							
EP 2.1.10 Engage, Assess, Intervene, and Evaluate with Individuals, Families, Groups, Organizations and Communities								
a.	Substantively and affectively prepare for action with individuals, families, groups, organizations, and communities							
b.	Use empathy and other interpersonal skills							
c.	Develop a mutually agreed-on focus of work and desired outcomes							
d.	Collect, organize, and interpret client data							
e.	Assess client strengths and limitations							
f.	Develop mutually agreed-on intervention goals and objectives							
g.	Select appropriate intervention strategies							
h.	Initiate actions to achieve organizational goals							
i.	Implement prevention interventions that enhance client capacities							
j.	Help clients resolve problems							
k.	Negotiate, mediate, and advocate for clients							
l.	Facilitate transitions and endings							
m.	Critically analyze, monitor, and evaluate interventions							

Chapter 4
Understanding Organizations

Competencies/Practice Behaviors Exercise 4.1
Comparing and Contrasting Organizational Theories

Focus Competencies or Practice Behaviors:
- EP 2.1.7a   Utilize conceptual frameworks to guide the processes of assessment, intervention, and evaluation

Instructions:

A.   Review the material on theoretical perspectives of organizations

B.   What are the primary concepts involved in each of the following theoretical perspectives on organizations?

C.   What are the similarities and differences among the six perspectives?

D.   Which theoretical perspective(s) is (are) best?   Explain why

---

ORGANIZATIONAL THEORIES

Classical organizational theories
- Scientific management theories
- Administrative theory of management
- Bureaucracy

Neoclassical organizational theories

Human relations theories

Feminist theories

The cultural perspective

Political-economy theory

The institutional perspective

Contingency theory

Culture-quality theories

Systems theories

Competencies/Practice Behaviors Exercise 4.2
Identifying and Evaluating Management Concepts

Focus Competencies or Practice Behaviors:
- EP 2.1.7a   Utilize conceptual frameworks to guide the processes of assessment, intervention, and evaluation

Instructions:

A.   Review the content on working in a bureaucracy and a total quality approach to management

B.   For each of the following brief descriptions of a management approach, answer the subsequent questions

> **Description A:** Agency management emphasizes that workers should be consistent in their service provision, responsive to clients, and readily available when needed.

1.   To what extent does this management approach reflect that of a traditional bureaucracy or total quality management?

2.   What more specific concepts inherent in traditional bureaucracy or total quality management are reflected and why?

3.   What are the pros and cons of this management approach?

49

1.   To what extent does this management approach reflect that of a traditional bureaucracy or total quality management?

2.   What more specific concepts inherent in traditional bureaucracy or total quality management are reflected and why?

3.   What are the pros and cons of this management approach?

1.   To what extent does this management approach reflect that of a traditional bureaucracy or total quality management?

2.   What more specific concepts inherent in traditional bureaucracy or total quality management are reflected and why?

3.   What are the pros and cons of this management approach?

Description D: The agency is made up of numerous highly specialized units assigned to perform specific job tasks. The intent is to have the service provision process run smoothly and get things done. The rules are there to help practitioners accomplish their tasks in designated and consistent ways. Allowing practitioners much of their own decision-making initiative only paves the way for mistakes.

1.   To what extent does this management approach reflect that of a traditional bureaucracy or total quality management?

2.   What more specific concepts inherent in traditional bureaucracy or total quality management are reflected and why?

3.   What are the pros and cons of this management approach?

Focus Competencies or Practice Behaviors:
- EP 2.1.7a   Utilize conceptual frameworks to guide the processes of assessment, intervention, and evaluation

Instructions:

A.   Review the content on organizational theories and concepts characterizing them

B.   Each concept listed below characterizes one of the following organizational theories:
- Classical organizational theories
- Neoclassical theories
- Human relations theories
- Feminist theories
- Cultural perspective
- Political-economy theory
- The institutional perspective
- Contingency theory
- Culture-quality theories
- Systems theories

C.   Identify the organizational theory each concept characterizes

D.   Explain the concept's significance to that theory and how it helps you understand organizational behavior

FOR INSTRUCTORS: ANSWERS CAN BE FOUND IN THE *INSTRUCTOR'S MANUAL* IN EXERCISE 4.4

1.   *Concept: Dependence on the external environment, the effects of resources and power, and power struggles*

Organizational theory it characterizes:

Explain the concept's significance for understanding the theory and organizational behavior:

2.   *Concept: Responses to social institutions and external pressures, and adherence to rules that implies legitimacy*

Organizational theory it characterizes:

Explain the concept's significance for understanding the theory and organizational behavior:

3.   *Concept: The personal is political*

Organizational theory it characterizes:

Explain the concept's significance for understanding the theory and organizational behavior:

4.   *Concept: Provision of inducements (incentives) to enhance contributions and motivation to perform*

Organizational theory it characterizes:

Explain the concept's significance for understanding the theory and organizational behavior:

5.   *Concept: Formal structure and close supervision of employees*

Organizational theory it characterizes:

Explain the concept's significance for understanding the theory and organizational behavior:

6.   *Concept: Use of different means to solve different problems with no one best way to accomplish goals*

Organizational theory it characterizes:

Explain the concept's significance for understanding the theory and organizational behavior:

7.   *Concept: All parts of the organization being related to all other parts, as the organization interacts with its environment*

Organizational theory it characterizes:

Explain the concept's significance for understanding the theory and organizational behavior:

8.   *Concept: Employee morale, employee productivity, motivation, and leadership*

Organizational theory it characterizes:

Explain the concept's significance for understanding the theory and organizational behavior:

9.   *Concept: An organization's unique mixture of values, standards, and presumptions about how things should be done as a context for work*

Organizational theory it characterizes:

Explain the concept's significance for understanding the theory and organizational behavior:

10.   *Concept: Development of a strong set of shared positive values and norms within an organization with emphasis on high quality production and high employee commitment*

Organizational theory it characterizes:

Explain the concept's significance for understanding the theory and organizational behavior:

Focus Competencies or Practice Behaviors:
- EP 2.1.7a   Utilize conceptual frameworks to guide the processes of assessment, intervention, and evaluation

Instructions:

A.   Review the concepts in the box below which are especially significant in understanding systems in the macro environment

---

SYSTEMS THEORIES' CONCEPTS

System: A set of orderly and interrelated elements that form a functional whole.

Boundaries: Borders or margins that separate one entity (for example, a system) from another. They enclose the repeatedly occurring patterns that characterize the relationships within a system and give that system a particular identity.

Subsystem: A secondary or subordinate system within a larger system.

Homeostasis: The tendency for a system to maintain a relatively stable, constant state of balance.

Role: The culturally established social behavior and conduct expected of a person having a designated status in a particular group or society.

Relationship: The dynamic interpersonal connection between two or more persons or systems that involves how they think about, feel about, and behave toward each other.

Output: What happens to input after it has been processed by some system.

Feedback: A special form of input where a system receives information about its own performance.

Negative feedback: Input to a system about negative aspects of functioning that enables that system to correct any deviations or mistakes and return to a more homeostatic state.

Positive feedback: Input to a system about what that system is doing correctly in order to maintain itself and thrive.

Interface: The contact point between various systems including individuals and organizations, where interaction and communication may take place.

Differentiation: A system's tendency to move from a more simplified to a more complex existence.

Entropy: The natural tendency of a system to progress toward disorganization, depletion, disintegration, and, in essence, death.

Negative entropy: The process of a system toward growth and development—the opposite of entropy.

Equifinality: The idea that there are many different means to the same end.

B.   Select a social services agency in your area and make an appointment to speak with a social worker or administrator. You may conduct the interview over the phone if necessary. Your goal is to better understand organizational functioning by applying a systems perspective. Ask the interviewee the following questions and record her or his responses. Note that the questions are rephrased in systems terms in parentheses.

C.   Write a 3 to 5 page paper summarizing the information you received using systems theories' concepts and terminology to describe the agency's functioning

1.   How is the agency structured—that is, what professional departments or units does it comprise *(what are its various subsystems)*? How many departments or units are there?

2.   How are professional departments or units defined *(what are their boundaries)*? Are they divided according to the problems they address—for example, all staff serving abused children under one umbrella? Or according to function—e.g., intake, assessment, referral, counseling? Or according to some combination of the two?

3.   Do you consider the agency relatively stable *(maintaining homeostasis)*? Are funding sources *(input)* stable? What are the primary funding sources for service provision?

4.   How is the effectiveness of service provision *(output)* measured?

5.   What types of *feedback* are solicited from consumers, such as clients or other agencies purchasing services?

6.   Has the agency recently received any *positive or negative feedback* about its effectiveness? If so, what was this feedback?

7.   Over time, has the agency become more complex—for example, added new services, served new client groups, or added new staff *(differentiation)*? If so, in what ways?

8.   Is the agency generally improving its ability to function and provide effective services *(negative entropy)*? Is it encountering increasing problems—for example, funding, regulations, or changing client needs *(entropy)*? In either case, in what ways?

Competencies/Practice Behaviors Exercise 4.5
Organizational Culture Investigation

Focus Competencies or Practice Behaviors:
- EP 2.1.7a   Utilize conceptual frameworks to guide the processes of assessment, intervention, and evaluation

Instructions:
A.   Review the concepts in the box below which are especially significant in understanding systems in the macro environment
B.   The two questionnaires below contain questions you can ask to evaluate organizational culture. They compare two organizational cultures—a traditional bureaucracy and a client/employee centered agency employing Total Quality Management (TQM) principles. This exercise will sensitize you to differences in organizational culture and to how those differences may affect you professionally
C.   Select a social services agency—large or small, public or private—in your area. You may interview a worker, a supervisor or agency administrator, or both a worker and an administrator. (If you choose this last option, you can compare their impressions of the organizational culture. Frequently, workers—who are in direct contact with clients and their views—perceive an organization very differently than do administrators—who are exposed to political, funding, and regulatory pressures from the external macro environment.) This questionnaire will not yield a

specific score to precisely define organizational culture, but it will provide you with some thought-provoking information about agency life

D. Instruct the interviewee(s) to answer both questionnaires to the best of her or his (their) ability, using this scale: (1) never; (2) infrequently; (3) sometimes; (4) frequently; and (5) always. Record the responses below

E. Add up the scores for each questionnaire separately and divide each by ten. The two average scores will range from 1—low organizational commitment to that management style, to 5—very high commitment to that management style. You may find an inverse relationship between scores on the Bureaucratic and Customer/Employee Orientation questionnaires, reflecting the extreme differences between the two

---

Bureaucratic Orientation Questionnaire[1]

1. Most professional employees in this organization hold a clearly defined job with clearly designated responsibilities.

Never	Infrequently	Sometimes	Frequently	Always
1	2	3	4	5

2. Most professional employees in this organization are told straightforwardly and specifically how their jobs should be accomplished.

Never	Infrequently	Sometimes	Frequently	Always
1	2	3	4	5

3. Supervisors closely scrutinize employees' work.

Never	Infrequently	Sometimes	Frequently	Always
1	2	3	4	5

4. The administration considers efficiency to be of the utmost importance.

Never	Infrequently	Sometimes	Frequently	Always
1	2	3	4	5

5. Decisions about agency policy and practice tend to be made by higher administration and flow from the top down.

Never	Infrequently	Sometimes	Frequently	Always
1	2	3	4	5

6. Power in the agency is held primarily by top executives.

---

[1]Many of the questions listed below are derived from the conflicts posed by Knopf (1979) that occur between the orientations of helping professionals and bureaucratic systems.

	Never	Infrequently	Sometimes	Frequently	Always
	1	2	3	4	5

7. Communication in the organization flows from the top down.

	Never	Infrequently	Sometimes	Frequently	Always
	1	2	3	4	5

8. There is little communication among horizontal units—that is, units of approximately equal status that perform different functions.

	Never	Infrequently	Sometimes	Frequently	Always
	1	2	3	4	5

9. The organization emphasizes a rigid structure of power and authority that works to maintain stability and the status quo.

	Never	Infrequently	Sometimes	Frequently	Always
	1	2	3	4	5

10. The organization and its administration place great importance on specified rules and policies and expect employees to adhere to them.

	Never	Infrequently	Sometimes	Frequently	Always
	1	2	3	4	5

TOTAL = _____ ÷ 10 = _____ **(AVERAGE SCORE)**

Customer/Employee Orientation Questionnaire

1. The organization places primary importance on the client (customer) and on effective service to clients.

	Never	Infrequently	Sometimes	Frequently	Always
	1	2	3	4	5

2. The organization holds in high regard practitioners who provide services directly to clients.

	Never	Infrequently	Sometimes	Frequently	Always
	1	2	3	4	5

3. The organization's administrative structure is viewed primarily as a support system for clients and direct service workers.

Never	Infrequently	Sometimes	Frequently	Always
1	2	3	4	5

4. The organization's administration considers quality of service—consistency of service provision, responsiveness to clients' needs, and service availability—its major goal.

Never	Infrequently	Sometimes	Frequently	Always
1	2	3	4	5

5. Organizational leadership seeks to empower agency practitioners so that they can do their jobs as effectively as possible.

Never	Infrequently	Sometimes	Frequently	Always
1	2	3	4	5

6. Professional employees are encouraged to provide input into how the organization is run.

Never	Infrequently	Sometimes	Frequently	Always
1	2	3	4	5

7. The organization values client feedback and incorporates it into improving service provision.

Never	Infrequently	Sometimes	Frequently	Always
1	2	3	4	5

8. Professional employees are encouraged to work together to improve service provision.

Never	Infrequently	Sometimes	Frequently	Always
1	2	3	4	5

9. Communication flow is open and frequent among most agency units.

Never	Infrequently	Sometimes	Frequently	Always
1	2	3	4	5

10. Professional employees feel that their input to upper levels of administration is valued and put to use.

Never	Infrequently	Sometimes	Frequently	Always
1	2	3	4	5

TOTAL = _____ ÷ **10** = _____ **(AVERAGE SCORE)**

F.   After calculating scores, explain to the interviewee(s) which organizational culture his agency reflects. Give brief examples of traditional bureaucracy and of TQM. Then ask the following questions about the organization's culture and effectiveness, and write a two- to four-page paper summarizing your findings
     1.   How would you describe the organization's culture?
     2.   To what extent do you feel the organization's culture enhances or detracts from practitioners' ability to do their work effectively?
     3.   What are the strengths of the organization's culture?
     4.   What are the weaknesses of the organization's culture?
     5.   Ideally, what changes, if any, would you make in the organizational culture?

Competencies/Practice Behaviors Exercise 4.6
Role Play The Learning Organization

Focus Competencies or Practice Behaviors:
   • EP 2.1.9a   Continuously discover, appraise, and attend to changing locales, populations, scientific and technological developments, and emerging societal trends to provide relevant services
   • EP 2.1.9b   Provide leadership in promoting sustainable changes in service delivery and practice to improve the quality of social services

Instructions:
A.   Review the management trend related to empowering workers described in the text as the learning organization, including the following concepts
     1.   Power is redistributed from higher levels to lower levels in the organizational structure through increased worker participation
     2.   Employees are encouraged to be creative and share their ideas with others
     3.   Clients' perceptions about services are sought out so that improvements in quality and effectiveness can be made
     4.   The use of teams are encouraged to make recommendations and decisions that management takes seriously and implements
     5.   Open information is promoted
     6.   Individuals are encouraged to lead because they want to serve one another as well as a higher purpose
B.   Role play the following scenario, with a classmate playing each of the "learning disabilities" from the text (in the second box below)

Learning Organization Scenario:

You have been hired by the board of directors of the Drearyland Community Action Program. This organization has historically been run as a traditional bureaucracy. Most of the employees have been there for many years and are entrenched in their individual idiosyncrasies.

You presented the board with your intended management of a learning organization. You defined such an organization as one "in which everyone is engaged in identifying and solving problems, enabling the organization to continuously experiment, change, and improve, thus increasing its capacity to grow, learn, and achieve its purpose" (Aldag & Kuzuhara, 2005; Daft, 2010a, p. 50).

The board was very receptive of your intention and wished you good luck! You were a little surprised by them wishing you good luck; however, you were ready to begin.

60

Your two Associate Directors are Bob Dolittle, who likes to be called "Bull," and you feel he is going to be your "go-to" guy who can really get things done. The other is Catastra Phee. You believe she is a team player and is quite interested in new changes in the agency.

After a few weeks, the following personalities began to make themselves known….

"Learning Disabilities" Caste of Characters:

Tunnela—She only focuses on the tasks required in her position. She neither feels part of the greater whole nor feels that she has input into the organization's vision for the future.

Blamican—His favorite line is "It's not my fault." It's always someone else's fault. He is constantly blaming others for the consequences of his own behavior.

"Bull"—He is a "take charge" kind of guy. He is forever lashing out at others while he is trying to solve problems.

Catastra—She is the queen of the "hidden agenda." She appears to be a team player, but is always undermining any new policy decision or new program development

---

C.   Your "team" is meeting to discuss why your new policy decisions and your new program development plans have become disasters.

1.   How do you deal with these personalities?

2.   What needs to be done in this agency? No, you can't fire them all and start over!

3.   How were the concepts of the learning organization helpful to you in working with this agency?

4.   Have your "employees" assess your ability as a manager in a learning organization.

Name: _____ **Date:** _____

Supervisor's Name: _____

Focus Competencies/Practice Behaviors:
- EP 2.1.7a   Utilize conceptual frameworks to guide the processes of assessment, intervention, and evaluation
- EP 2.1.9a   Continuously discover, appraise, and attend to changing locales, populations, scientific and technological developments, and emerging societal trends to provide relevant services
- EP 2.1.9b   Provide leadership in promoting sustainable changes in service delivery and practice to improve the quality of social services

Instructions:

A.   Evaluate your work or your partner's work in the Focus Competencies/Practice Behaviors by completing the Competencies/Practice Behaviors Assessment form below

B.   What other Competencies/Practice Behaviors did you use to complete these Exercises? Be sure to record them in your assessments

1.	I have attained this competency/practice behavior (in the range of 81 to 100%)
2.	I have largely attained this competency/practice behavior (in the range of 61 to 80%)
3.	I have partially attained this competency/practice behavior (in the range of 41 to 60%)
4.	I have made a little progress in attaining this competency/practice behavior (in the range of 21 to 40%)
5.	I have made almost no progress in attaining this competency/practice behavior (in the range of 0 to 20%)

EPAS 2008 Core Competencies & Core Practice Behaviors	Student Self Assessment						Evaluator Feedback
Student and Evaluator Assessment Scale and Comments	0	1	2	3	4	5	Agree/Disagree/Comments
EP 2.1.1 Identify as a Professional Social Worker and Conduct Oneself Accordingly							
a. Advocate for client access to the services of social work							
b. Practice personal reflection and self-correction to assure continual professional development							
c. Attend to professional roles and boundaries							
d. Demonstrate professional demeanor in behavior, appearance, and communication							
e. Engage in career-long learning							
f. Use supervision and consultation							
EP 2.1.2 Apply Social Work Ethical Principles to Guide Professional Practice							
a. Recognize and manage personal values in a way that allows professional values to guide practice							
b. Make ethical decisions by applying NASW Code of Ethics and, as applicable, of the IFSW/IASSW Ethics in Social Work, Statement of Principles							
c. Tolerate ambiguity in resolving ethical conflicts							
d. Apply strategies of ethical reasoning to arrive at principled decisions							

EP 2.1.3 Apply Critical Thinking to Inform and Communicate Professional Judgments								
a.	Distinguish, appraise, and integrate multiple sources of knowledge, including research-based knowledge and practice wisdom							
b.	Analyze models of assessment, prevention, intervention, and evaluation							
c.	Demonstrate effective oral and written communication in working with individuals, families, groups, organizations, communities, and colleagues							
EP 2.1.4 Engage Diversity and Difference in Practice								
a.	Recognize the extent to which a culture's structures and values may oppress, marginalize, alienate, or create or enhance privilege and power							
b.	Gain sufficient self-awareness to eliminate the influence of personal biases and values in working with diverse groups							
c.	Recognize and communicate their understanding of the importance of difference in shaping life experiences							
d.	View themselves as learners and engage those with whom they work as informants							
EP 2.1.5 Advance Human Rights and Social and Economic Justice								
a.	Understand forms and mechanisms of oppression and discrimination							
b.	Advocate for human rights and social and economic justice							
c.	Engage in practices that advance social and economic justice							
EP 2.1.6 Engage in Research-Informed Practice and Practice-Informed Research								
a.	Use practice experience to inform scientific inquiry							
b.	Use research evidence to inform practice							
EP 2.1.7 Apply Knowledge of Human Behavior and the Social Environment								
a.	Utilize conceptual frameworks to guide the processes of assessment, intervention, and evaluation							
b.	Critique and apply knowledge to understand person and environment							
EP 2.1.8 Engage in Policy Practice to Advance Social and Economic Well-Being and to Deliver Effective Social Work Services								
a.	Analyze, formulate, and advocate for policies that advance social well-being							
b.	Collaborate with colleagues and clients for effective policy action							
EP 2.1.9 Respond to Contexts that Shape Practice								
a.	Continuously discover, appraise, and attend to changing locales, populations, scientific and technological developments, and emerging societal trends to provide relevant services							
b.	Provide leadership in promoting sustainable							

63

changes in service delivery and practice to improve the quality of social services								
EP 2.1.10 Engage, Assess, Intervene, and Evaluate with Individuals, Families, Groups, Organizations and Communities								
a.	Substantively and affectively prepare for action with individuals, families, groups, organizations, and communities							
b.	Use empathy and other interpersonal skills							
c.	Develop a mutually agreed-on focus of work and desired outcomes							
d.	Collect, organize, and interpret client data							
e.	Assess client strengths and limitations							
f.	Develop mutually agreed-on intervention goals and objectives							
g.	Select appropriate intervention strategies							
h.	Initiate actions to achieve organizational goals							
i.	Implement prevention interventions that enhance client capacities							
j.	Help clients resolve problems							
k.	Negotiate, mediate, and advocate for clients							
l.	Facilitate transitions and endings							
m.	Critically analyze, monitor, and evaluate interventions							

Chapter 5
PREPARE—Decision Making for Organizational Change

Competencies/Practice Behaviors Exercise 5.1
Identifying Leadership Styles of Decision-Makers

Focus Competencies or Practice Behaviors:
- EP 2.1.9b   Provide leadership in promoting sustainable changes in service delivery and practice to improve the quality of social services

Instructions:

A.   Review the material on leadership styles of decision-makers provided in the text

B.   Match the following leadership styles with the descriptions cited below. Note that some descriptions may apply to more than one leadership style

               1. Climber
               2. Conserver
               3. Zealot
               4. Advocate
               5. Statesperson

---

1.   A leader who is more concerned with the welfare of society as a whole than with the agency or a particular client population.

    a.   What leadership style(s) characterize(s) this leader?

    b.   Explain why.

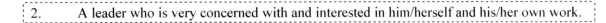

2.   A leader who is very concerned with and interested in him/herself and his/her own work.

    a.   What leadership style(s) characterize(s) this leader?

    b.   Explain why.

3.   A leader who likes to closely control subordinates to ensure nobody else is seen as a rising star.

   a.   What leadership style(s) characterize(s) this leader?

   b.   Explain why.

4.   A leader who has exceptionally high commitment to the goals of the organization or unit of which she or he is a member.

   a.   What leadership style(s) characterize(s) this leader?

   b.   Explain why.

5.   A leader who is a superduper go-getter, exudes energy, and loves creative innovation.

   a.   What leadership style(s) characterize(s) this leader?

   b.   Explain why.

6.   A leader who is a skilled administrator and is exceptionally committed to the agency and its clients.

   a.   What leadership style(s) characterize(s) this leader?

   b.   Explain why.

7.   A leader who will probably not support subordinates' ideas for change, but might just confiscate them and take them as her/his own.

   a.   What leadership style(s) characterize(s) this leader?

   b.   Explain why.

8.   A leader who is not so much concerned about quality of service provision as following the rules to the letter.

   a.   What leadership style(s) characterize(s) this leader?

   b.   Explain why.

9.   A leader who has excellent public relations skills but is not very good at attending to detail or carrying through with long-term proposals.

   a.   What leadership style(s) characterize(s) this leader?

   b.   Explain why.

10.   A leader who will probably not spend much time listening to your ideas.

   a.   What leadership style(s) characterize(s) this leader?

   b.   Explain why.

C.   After completing above exercise, answer the following questions

        1.   In what ways are these five leadership styles different?

        2.   In what ways are these five leadership styles similar?

        3.   What is the ideal leadership style? How does it differ from any or all of these?

Competencies/Practice Behaviors Exercise 5.2
Evaluating Personal Characteristics for Macro Practice

Focus Competencies or Practice Behaviors:
- EP 2.1.1b   Practice personal reflection and self-correction to assure continual professional development

Instructions:
A.   Review the material on PREPARE including the various substeps involved
B.   Evaluating your own characteristics, strengths, and weaknesses is as important in macro practice as in micro or mezzo practice. Indeed, macro practice skills are built upon micro and mezzo practice skills, and you will use the same interpersonal skills in macro practice as you do at the other levels. Picture yourself working with staff, administrators, and clients in an agency. Answer the questions and follow the instructions below

68

1. Complete the following four "Who are you?" statements, using adjectives, nouns, or phrases. If you had to summarize who you are, what would you say?

I am

I am

I am

I am

2. What adjectives would you use to describe yourself? Circle all that apply

Happy	Sad	Honest	Dishonest	Sensitive
Insensitive	Trustworthy	Untrustworthy	Caring	Uncaring
Outgoing	Shy	Withdrawn	Friendly	Unfriendly
Religious	Not-very-religious	Nervous	Calm	Formal
Informal	Aggressive	Assertive	Timid	Confident
Not-very-confident	Careful	Careless	Capable	Incapable
Independent	Dependent	Affectionate	Cool	Wary
Bold	Cheerful	Witty	Unassuming	Thorough
Easy-going	Determined	Clever	Responsive	Strong-minded
Leisurely	Industrious	Weak-willed (at least sometimes)	Controlled	Spontaneous
Serious	Funny	Tough	Pleasant	Daring
Eager	Efficient	Not-so-efficient	Artistic	Tactful
Intolerant	Vulnerable	Likable	Smart	Understanding
Impatient	Patient	Imaginative	Wordy	Concise
Open-minded	Funny	Organized	Somewhat-disorganized	Conscientious
Late	Emotional	Unemotional	Controlled	Open
Creative	Curious	Sincere	Precise	A-little-haphazard
Cooperative	Ethical	Brave	Mature	Spunky

3. Cite your four greatest strengths—personal qualities, talents, or accomplishments.

Strength A

Strength B

69

Strength   C

Strength   D

4.   Several weaknesses are listed below. To what extent do you suffer from each? Rate yourself on each one by placing the appropriate number beside it.

1. Very serious   2. Moderately serious   3. Mildly serious   4. Not at all serious

Lack of understanding of community service system   _____
Personal stress   _____
Exhaustion and fatigue   _____
Over-involvement with job   _____
Insufficient time   _____
Lack of self-confidence   _____

5.   Cite your four greatest weaknesses.

Weakness   A

Weakness   B

Weakness   C

Weakness   D

6.   How do you think your personal strengths will help you work with other staff, administrators, and clients in macro practice situations?

7.   What weaknesses, if any, do you think you need to address to improve your ability to work with staff, administrators, and clients in macro practice situations?

Competencies/Practice Behaviors Exercise 5.3
Adapting PREPARE to a Case Example: Empowerment for Women of Color

---

Focus Competencies or Practice Behaviors:
- EP 2.1.4a   Recognize the extent to which a culture's structures and values may oppress, marginalize, alienate, or create or enhance privilege and power
- EP 2.1.10a   Substantively and affectively prepare for action with individuals, families, groups, organizations, and communities
- EP 2.1.10d   Collect, organize, and interpret client data

Instructions:
A.   Review the PREPARE process in detail
B.   Read the following case vignette and answer the subsequent questions using each step of the PREPARE process. Feel free to add creative ideas and solutions to each phase of the decision-making process

> ***CASE EXAMPLE:*** You are a social worker for Shatterproof County Department of Social Services in the Public Assistance Division.[1] Shatterproof is a huge urban county populated primarily by people of color. Following the demise of Aid to Families with Dependent Children (AFDC),[2] your agency is struggling to adapt to new policies, regulations, and requirements concerning the distribution of clients' needed resources. You and your colleagues are working to adjust and conform to new expectations. However, that is not the immediate focus of your concern.

---

[1] *Public assistance* is financial benefits and in-kind (services of goods versus cash) benefits provided to people who can't support themselves.

[2] *AFDC* is "a former public assistance program, originating in the Social Security Act as Aid to Dependent Children. It was funded by the federal and state governments to provide financial aid for needy children who are deprived of parental support because of death, incapacitation, or absence" (Barker, 2003, p. 14).

In working for the county these past three years, you have become increasingly disturbed about the way many workers treat clients, most of whom are women of color. You feel that workers are pressured to process clients through the problem-solving process as quickly as possible and that too little emphasis is placed on client empowerment. *Empowerment* is the "process of increasing personal, interpersonal, or political power so that individuals can take action to improve their life situations" (Gutierrez, 1995, p. 205).[3] You feel strongly that if workers assumed an empowerment-oriented approach, more clients would be able to gain control of the solutions to their own problems. Such an approach might involve teaching workers how to focus on empowerment approaches and techniques, including "accepting the client's definition of the problem," "identifying and building upon existing strengths," engaging in a realistic assessment of the client's power in her personal situation, "teaching specific skills" (such as "skills for community or organizational change; life skills," such as parenting, job seeking, and self-defense; and interpersonal skills, such as assertiveness, social competency, and self-advocacy), and "mobilizing resources and advocating for clients" (Gutierrez, 1995, pp. 208-10).

So you begin to wonder what you might be able to do about this situation. Clients ought to be allowed more input into the definition and solution of their problems, but workers are not as receptive to clients as they should be. Adopting an empowerment approach could greatly help in successfully implementing the new public assistance programs. Of course, this is not the agency's only problem. Workers are overly burdened with paperwork, and computers and programs are already outdated. Nevertheless, in your mind empowerment remains the dominant issue. You think social workers, supervisors, and administrators should be educated about empowerment issues and trained to implement empowerment approaches in practice. Emphasis should be placed on both empowerment values and skills. How can you increase awareness and implementation of a philosophy of empowerment in your huge agency? Upper-level administrators seem to inhabit some unreachable plane. There are only so many hours in your workday. What are your options? Can you start small by trying to reach workers in your own unit? (There are seven of you who report to one supervisor.) Can you initiate training for yourself and the other six workers in your unit?

Will the unit and the agency accept an empowerment approach? What factors will help you and what will hinder you? What will training the unit staff cost? The agency may have some funding available to provide in-service training for workers,[4] because it does require every worker to complete continuing education units (CEUs)[5] on a regular basis. As a matter of fact, you have a flier announcing an empowerment training seminar led by an expert in the field. You also know of a social work professor in the local university who might be able to do some training or to refer you to someone who can. What would that cost? Is there any possibility of getting volunteers to do the training on a limited basis?

Are there other potential barriers to training besides cost? Certainly the agency's CEU requirements are in your favor. Although the agency is in some turmoil due to new programs and requirements, it seems there has always been some degree of hubbub. That's really nothing new. Training a single unit is a relatively small task. Ideally, you'd like to include the entire agency, but that's something to think about in the future. You can think of no one outside the agency who would actively oppose your plan.

---

[3] Many of the concepts presented here are taken from L. M. Gutierrez (1995). "Working with women of color: An empowerment perspective." In J. Rothman, J. L. Erlich, & J.E. Tropman (eds.), *Strategies of Community Intervention* (pp. 204-220). Itasca, IL: F. E. Peacock.

[4] *In-service training programs* are educational sessions provided by an agency for its staff to develop their skills or improve their effectiveness.

[5] Acquiring CEUs often involves successful completion of "qualified academic or professional courses" (Barker, 1995, p. 79). One intent is to keep professionals in a range of professions updated with current knowledge relevant to their fields.

Do you think you can "pull off" such a project, even though training programs aren't in your job description? What personal characteristics will work to your advantage in the process? For example, are you capable, responsible, and/or assertive? Do you have exceptionally strong communication or negotiation skills? On the other hand, what weaknesses do you have that might act against a successful change process? For example, is it difficult for you to ask for things? Do you consider yourself shy or lacking in confidence?

The bottom line is that you really want other workers to work with clients more effectively by adopting an empowerment approach. Your goal, then, is to figure out how to provide training to help them do just that. You've discussed the idea with colleagues who seemed mildly positive about it. You don't think they'd be willing to take on primary responsibilities for the project, but it would be worthwhile speaking with some of them further.

Your colleague and friend Ortrude has some difficulties organizing and following through on details, but she usually speaks up for anything she believes in. Maybe you can win her support. There is also Virgilia, a hard-working, responsible worker who usually keeps her opinions to herself. You don't feel you know her very well, but she might be in favor of your idea. On the downside, there's your colleague and non-friend Bentley who typically "pooh-poohs" any innovative idea.

The agency's voluntary In-service Training Committee suggests and plans training for various agency units, so you will have to approach its members, and they might be supportive—even though their funding is limited and fluctuating. Since you don't personally know any committee members, you have no natural "in."

As to people in the community, you've already established that at least one expert is available (though you don't know what her fee would be) and that the professor at the university is another possibility.

What about your own position and how initiating such a project might affect you both professionally and personally. Your supervisor Astral is a "laid-back" type who generally gets her work done in a leisurely fashion. (Actually, you think she's kind of "spacey.") She is not someone to depend upon for high-powered consultations or for strong support for this initiative. On the other hand, if you're willing to do the work yourself, she will probably approve the project and send it up for higher level authorization. All agency in-service training must be approved by the agency's Assistant Director, Harvey. You think Harvey, a scrooge-like accountant at heart, is more likely to approve such a plan if it isn't extremely costly.

1. Answer the following questions with respect to this case example.

Exercise 5.4 (1):

Step 1: Identify Problems to Address
Substep 1.1: Evaluate the potential for macro level intervention. Discuss the seriousness of the identified problem situation in the case example above. In your own words, describe what you see as the core issue(s).

Substep 1.2: Define and prioritize the problems you've identified in the case example.

Substep 1.3: Translate problems into needs.

Substep 1.4: Determine which need or needs you will address if you are in this worker's situation.

Exercise 5.4 (2):

<u>**Step 2: Review Your Macro and Personal Reality**</u>
Substep 2.1: Evaluate the organizational and other macro variables potentially working for or against you in the macro change process as portrayed in the above case example. Fill out Figure 5.3, then explain the reasons for your responses below.

Figure 5.3: PREPARE--Evaluate Your Professional and Personal Risk

To what extent are you in danger of:	No danger	Some danger	Moderate danger	Serious danger
1. losing your job?				
2. decreasing your potential for upward mobility?				
3. seriously straining work relationships?				

Explain the reasons for your responses.

Substep 2.2: Assess your personal reality—that is, the strengths and weaknesses that may act for or against a successful change effort.

75

Exercise 5.4 (3):

Step 3: Establish Primary Goals
List the goals you would pursue if you were in the position described above.

Exercise 5.4 (4):

Step 4: Identify Relevant People of Influence

In the following Figure, list individuals and groups both inside and outside of the agency.

Figure 5.4: PREPARE--Identify Relevant **People** of Influence

Potential Action Systems	Name	Potential Support			
		Very good	Mildly good	Mildly bad	Very bad
Individuals in the Organization					
Groups in the Organization					
Individuals in the Community					
Groups in the the Community					
Others					

Give a brief explanation of your choices.

Exercise 5.4 (5):

Step 5: Assess Potential Financial Costs and Potential Benefits to Clients and Agency
Use the case example in your response.

Exercise 5.4 (6):

Step 6: Review Professional and Personal Risk
Could you lose your job, decrease your potential for upward mobility, and/or seriously strain your work relationships?

Exercise 5.4 (7):

Step 7: Evaluate the Potential Success of a Macro Change Process
Substep 7.1: Review (and summarize) **the prior PREPARE process, and weigh the pros and cons of proceeding with the macro change process.**

PROS
Client need (see Step 1):

Positive organizational and other macro variables (see Step 2):

Your own strengths (see Step 2):

Potential support (see Step 4):

Financial benefits (see Step 5):

CONS
Negative organizational and other macro variables (see Step 2):

Your own weaknesses (see Step 2):

Potential resistance (see Step 4):

Financial costs (see Step 5):

Your risks (see Step 6):

Substep 7.2: Identify possible macro approaches to use in the case example and determine how you would proceed (that is, continue the macro change process, postpone it, or drop the whole idea).

Focus Competencies or Practice Behaviors:
- EP 2.1.10g   Select appropriate intervention strategies

Instructions:

A.   Below are three case scenarios that might involve project implementation, program development, or policy change. For each, determine what type of change should be pursued, provide a rationale for your answer, and discuss potential benefits and problems of this change

---

Case Scenario A: You are the social worker at an elementary school. You notice that an increasing number of children come from turbulent homes. With each passing year these children present more problems with truancy. Their grades deteriorate and their illicit drug use soars. They need help. But what kind? Your job is to intervene individually with children suffering the most severe crises. You do some individual counseling, make some family visits, run a few support and treatment groups, and attend numerous assessment and planning meetings.

In a social work journal, you read about a new type of alternative approach for children at risk for the very problems you're seeing. One idea in particular catches your eye: A school in Illinois developed a "Friendship System" for children-at-risk. Volunteers solicited from among social work students at a nearby university attended a dozen training sessions, learning how to deal with these children. Each volunteer was then paired with a child and became the child's "special friend." The required commitment period was one year. Volunteers' responsibilities included spending time with the child at least once a week, being available when the child needed to talk, and generally being a positive role model for the child.

The program seems similar to Big Brothers/Big Sisters in which volunteers "work under professional supervision, usually by social workers, providing individual guidance and companionship to boys and girls deprived of a parent" (Barker, 1995, p. 35). But children in the Friendship System might or might not be from single-parent homes. The Friendship System's only prerequisite for the children is that school staff designate them as at-risk of problems including truancy, deteriorating school performance, and drug use, and school staff have substantial latitude in determining a child's eligibility for the program. Typical criteria include a recent divorce in the family, extreme shyness and withdrawal, academic problems, or other social problems. You think, "Wouldn't it be great if my school system had something like that in operation?"

What type of change would you consider pursuing—implementing a project, developing a program, or changing a school policy? Provide a rationale for the proposed change and discuss its potential benefits and problems.

---

1.   What type of change should be pursued?

2.   Explain your reasons for choosing this change.

3.   What are the potential benefits and problems of this change?

Case Scenario B: Your agency requires clients to fill out a 27-page admissions form before they can receive services. A large percentage of the agency's clients are Hispanic, and they speak very little English so the admissions form effectively prohibits Hispanic clients from receiving service. Because of the language difference, the agency blocks clients from receiving service.

What type of change would you consider pursuing—implementing a project, developing a program, or changing an agency policy? Provide a rationale for the proposed change and discuss its potential benefits and problems.

---

1.   What type of change should be pursued?

2.   Explain your reasons for choosing this change

3.   What are the potential benefits and problems of this change?

Case Scenario C: You are a social worker in a rural county social services agency. The towns within the county range in size from 1500 to 10,000 people, and the area has become increasingly impoverished as a number of small cheese and leather factories have left the area. Many people are struggling to survive in old shacks with little clothing and food. You know you can't overhaul the entire public assistance system, but you would like to initiate a food drive or collection to temporarily relieve people's suffering.

What type of change would you consider pursuing—implementing a project, developing a program, or changing an agency policy? Provide a rationale for the proposed change and discuss its potential benefits and problems.

---

1.   What type of change should be pursued?

2.   Explain your reasons for choosing this change.

3.   What are the potential benefits and problems of this change?

Focus Competencies or Practice Behaviors:
- EP 2.1.9b   Provide leadership in promoting sustainable changes in service delivery and practice to improve the quality of social services

Instructions:
A.   Review the material on leadership styles of decision-makers provided in the text
B.   Five classmates will each receive one of the following definitions of leadership styles by copying, cutting them, and distributing them
C.   The rest of the class will participate as the team involved in the preparations for the food drive
D.   Case Scenario C from the previous exercise is provided below, along with the additional information that you have been given the go-ahead to initiate the food drive

> ***Case Scenario C:*** You are a social worker in a rural county social services agency. The towns within the county range in size from 1500 to 10,000 people, and the area has become increasingly impoverished as a number of small cheese and leather factories have left the area. Many people are struggling to survive in old shacks with little clothing and food. You know you can't overhaul the entire public assistance system, but you have been given permission to initiate a food drive or collection to temporarily relieve people's suffering.
>
> There is so much to do now. You and your team must begin these preparations. Your team is so overworked as it is, but this is a project will help the community, the agency's clients, and the agency itself.

E.   One at a time, each of the five "leaders" will portray their particular leadership style by starting this first meeting to begin the preparations for the food drive

> You are the **Statesperson** who is more concerned with the welfare of society as a whole than with the agency or a particular client population. One of your strengths lies in establishing excellent public relations with others; however, you are not good at attending to detail and carrying through on long-term proposals.

> You will portray the **Climber** who tends to closely control subordinates to ensure nobody else is seen as a rising star. You are sometimes referred to as "the narcissist." You tend to interpret any bright ideas on your subordinates' part as threatening to your own status. Sometimes you even confiscate their ideas and take it as your own.

> Your leadership style is called the **Zealot**. You are a go-getter who exudes energy and loves creative innovation. You are very preoccupied with yourself. You think you know best, regardless of others' opinions. You expect subordinates to be your faithful devotees. You may or may not listen to a macro change proposal, depending on how it fits into your view of the universe.

You are the **Conserver**. You toil to preserve the homeostatic status quo. You are very concerned with and interested in yourself and your work. You are sometimes called a "typical bureaucrat." You love filling out forms on a routine and timely basis. You tend to be a strong proponent of goal displacement: Quality of service is not of much concern to you unless it involves your higher priority of following the rules. You generally abhor fresh and innovative ideas that might disrupt the steady flow of paperwork.

Your role is the **Advocate.** You are a person who has exceptionally high commitment to the goals of the organization or unit of which you are a member, or to a client population serviced by the agency. You are a skilled administrator. You can protect your corner of the agency from such external threats as funding cuts and can mediate disputes among your own staff. You are generally straight-forward, primarily concerned about the well-being of both clients and agency. You are the most likely to work toward the benefit of the agency and its clients. You are least likely to put your egos first or to steal your ideas.

F.   Assess how each "leader" performed her or his role, as well as how the class responded to each leadership style. Which style received the most effort from the team? Which style would you like to see as your leader? Which style do you see yourself portraying when you become a leader of a team?

Chapter 5 Competencies or Practice Behaviors Exercises Assessment:

Name: _____ **Date:** _____

Supervisor's Name: _____

Focus Competencies/Practice Behaviors:

- EP 2.1.1b   Practice personal reflection and self-correction to assure continual professional development
- EP 2.1.4a   Recognize the extent to which a culture's structures and values may oppress, marginalize, alienate, or create or enhance privilege and power
- EP 2.1.9b   Provide leadership in promoting sustainable changes in service delivery and practice to improve the quality of social services
- EP 2.1.10a   Substantively and affectively prepare for action with individuals, families, groups, organizations, and communities
- EP 2.1.10d   Collect, organize, and interpret client data
- EP 2.1.10g   Select appropriate intervention strategies

Instructions:

A.   Evaluate your work or your partner's work in the Focus Competencies/Practice Behaviors by completing the Competencies/Practice Behaviors Assessment form below

B.   What other Competencies/Practice Behaviors did you use to complete these Exercises? Be sure to record them in your assessments

1.	I have attained this competency/practice behavior (in the range of 81 to 100%)
2.	I have largely attained this competency/practice behavior (in the range of 61 to 80%)
3.	I have partially attained this competency/practice behavior (in the range of 41 to 60%)
4.	I have made a little progress in attaining this competency/practice behavior (in the range of 21 to 40%)
5.	I have made almost no progress in attaining this competency/practice behavior (in the range of 0 to 20%)

EPAS 2008 Core Competencies & Core Practice Behaviors	Student Self Assessment						Evaluator Feedback
Student and Evaluator Assessment Scale and Comments	0	1	2	3	4	5	Agree/Disagree/Comments
EP 2.1.1 Identify as a Professional Social Worker and Conduct Oneself Accordingly							
a. Advocate for client access to the services of social work							
b. Practice personal reflection and self-correction to assure continual professional development							
c. Attend to professional roles and boundaries							
d. Demonstrate professional demeanor in behavior, appearance, and communication							
e. Engage in career-long learning							
f. Use supervision and consultation							
EP 2.1.2 Apply Social Work Ethical Principles to Guide Professional Practice							
a. Recognize and manage personal values in a way that allows professional values to guide practice							
b. Make ethical decisions by applying NASW Code of Ethics and, as applicable, of the							

85

IFSW/IASSW Ethics in Social Work, Statement of Principles							
c. Tolerate ambiguity in resolving ethical conflicts							
d. Apply strategies of ethical reasoning to arrive at principled decisions							
EP 2.1.3 Apply Critical Thinking to Inform and Communicate Professional Judgments							
a. Distinguish, appraise, and integrate multiple sources of knowledge, including research-based knowledge and practice wisdom							
b. Analyze models of assessment, prevention, intervention, and evaluation							
c. Demonstrate effective oral and written communication in working with individuals, families, groups, organizations, communities, and colleagues							
EP 2.1.4 Engage Diversity and Difference in Practice							
a. Recognize the extent to which a culture's structures and values may oppress, marginalize, alienate, or create or enhance privilege and power							
b. Gain sufficient self-awareness to eliminate the influence of personal biases and values in working with diverse groups							
c. Recognize and communicate their understanding of the importance of difference in shaping life experiences							
d. View themselves as learners and engage those with whom they work as informants							
EP 2.1.5 Advance Human Rights and Social and Economic Justice							
a. Understand forms and mechanisms of oppression and discrimination							
b. Advocate for human rights and social and economic justice							
c. Engage in practices that advance social and economic justice							
EP 2.1.6 Engage in Research-Informed Practice and Practice-Informed Research							
a. Use practice experience to inform scientific inquiry							
b. Use research evidence to inform practice							
EP 2.1.7 Apply Knowledge of Human Behavior and the Social Environment							
a. Utilize conceptual frameworks to guide the processes of assessment, intervention, and evaluation							
b. Critique and apply knowledge to understand person and environment							
EP 2.1.8 Engage in Policy Practice to Advance Social and Economic Well-Being and to Deliver Effective Social Work Services							
a. Analyze, formulate, and advocate for policies that advance social well-being							
b. Collaborate with colleagues and clients for effective policy action							

EP 2.1.9 Respond to Contexts that Shape Practice							
a. Continuously discover, appraise, and attend to changing locales, populations, scientific and technological developments, and emerging societal trends to provide relevant services							
b. Provide leadership in promoting sustainable changes in service delivery and practice to improve the quality of social services							
EP 2.1.10 Engage, Assess, Intervene, and Evaluate with Individuals, Families, Groups, Organizations and Communities							
a. Substantively and affectively prepare for action with individuals, families, groups, organizations, and communities							
b. Use empathy and other interpersonal skills							
c. Develop a mutually agreed-on focus of work and desired outcomes							
d. Collect, organize, and interpret client data							
e. Assess client strengths and limitations							
f. Develop mutually agreed-on intervention goals and objectives							
g. Select appropriate intervention strategies							
h. Initiate actions to achieve organizational goals							
i. Implement prevention interventions that enhance client capacities							
j. Help clients resolve problems							
k. Negotiate, mediate, and advocate for clients							
l. Facilitate transitions and endings							
m. Critically analyze, monitor, and evaluate interventions							

Competencies/Practice Behaviors Exercise 6.1
Targeting Policies for Change

Focus Competencies or Practice Behaviors:
- EP 2.1.8a   Analyze, formulate, and advocate for policies that advance social well-being

Instructions:
A.   Review the IMAGINE process and the material on changing agency policy
B.   Identify a university, college, or department policy that you would like to see changed. This might involve anything from parking fees to grading procedures to the department's course prerequisites
C.   Follow the first four steps in the IMAGINE process for pursuing the designated policy change. The model is outlined below in the box

---

An Outline of the First Four Steps in the Imagine Process: Pursuing Policy Change

IMAGINE Step 1: Develop an Innovative **Idea.**
IMAGINE Step 2: **Muster** support and formulate an action system.
    Identify the macro client system.
    Identify the change agent system.
    Identify the target system.
    Identify the action system.
IMAGINE Step 3: Identify **assets.**
IMAGINE Step 4: Specify **goals** and action steps to attain them.

D.   Address the following questions:
    1.   What difficulties were you faced with in trying to follow the steps?

    2.   What additional information would be helpful?

    3.   What have you learned about changing policy from this experience?

Focus Competencies or Practice Behaviors:
- EP 2.1.7a   Utilize conceptual frameworks to guide the processes of assessment, intervention, and evaluation

Instructions:

A.   Review the material on macro client, action, and target systems

B.   Read the following vignette and identify the systems involved

---

Case Scenario: You are a hospital social worker who works with patients in the geriatric unit. Their problems typically include broken bones, onset of diseases such as diabetes, increasing mental confusion, and many accompanying physical difficulties. Patients usually remain hospitalized two days to two weeks. Most patients come to the hospital from their homes, and your job often involves placing patients in more structured settings because injuries or diseases have restricted their ability to function independently. Many are placed in health care centers (nursing homes).

You have been assigned Olga, 82, who fell and broke her hip. She also has diabetes and is increasingly incontinent. Prior to her fall, she barely subsisted in a second story one-room apartment, dependent on her monthly Social Security check for survival, and she has consumed all of her meager savings. She is an extremely pleasant woman who continues to emphasize that she doesn't want to be a burden on anyone. All of her family are dead. You worry that placement in an inferior setting will be tortuous for her if she doesn't receive the relatively intensive care she needs.

You notice that nursing homes vary dramatically in their levels of care, their appearance, the attention they give to patients, their ratios of staff to patients, the activities they offer, and their overall cleanliness. Patients with private insurance can easily enter one of the better facilities, while impoverished patients on Medicaid must go to inferior settings. You consider this both unfair and unethical.

You see yourself as a possible change agent. At least three of your colleagues in the hospital's social work unit have similar concerns about their own clients and the hospital's older adult clients in general. Your immediate supervisor is not really an "eager beaver" when it comes to initiating change, but you think you might be able to solicit some support from her. You are not certain whether upper levels of hospital administration believe that nursing home conditions are any of their business. In your state all nursing homes must be licensed, but licensing regulations require the maintenance of only the most minimal standards.

---

1.   Identify the macro client system in this case.

2.   Who might make up the action system?

3.   Who might be your target system?

Focus Competencies or Practice Behaviors:
- EP 2.1.10e   Assess client strengths and limitations

Instructions:

A.   Review the content on assets. Step 3 in the IMAGINE process involves the identification of assets. Whatever the type of macro level change, a change agent must determine what *assets* are available to implement the change. *Assets* are any resources and any advantages you have that will help in your proposed change process. Assets can include readily available funding, personnel who are able and willing to devote their time to implementing the change, and office space from which the change activities can be managed

B.   Read the following case scenario and identify the assets it reveals

> ***Case Scenario:*** Louise, a financial counselor at a private mental health agency, knows that the agency has access to special funding through personal donations made on behalf of persons "with special needs." She is not certain how the administration defines "special needs." But since the agency is privately owned, it is not subject to the same requirements and regulations that would limit a public agency. Louise learned about this special fund via the informal agency grapevine. It has never been publicly announced.
>
> Louise is working with several families whom she feels are in exceptional need. Their problems—including unemployment, depression, mental illness, poverty, unwanted pregnancy, and truancy—make them truly multiproblem families. Neither her agency nor any local public agency has been able to provide adequate resources for these families. Louise has established clear documentation of their extreme circumstances.
>
> Having worked at the agency for eight years, she feels she has gained substantial respect for her work and her ideas. She knows one member of the agency's board of directors fairly well, because she's worked with him on several projects in the past. (A board of directors is "a group of people empowered to establish an organization's objectives and policies and to oversee the activities of the personnel responsible for day-to-day implementation of those policies," and board members are often highly respected and influential volunteers from the community (Barker, 1995, p. 39). Louise might be able to contact this man to get information about the special-needs funding.
>
> She is aware, however, that her agency administration discourages workers from seeking access to this "secret" fund. Amounts available are limited, so the administration must dispense these funds extremely cautiously. In any case, Louise decides to approach the agency's Executive Director and request funding for the families in need.

1.   Identify the assets available to Louise.

Focus Competencies or Practice Behaviors:
- EP 2.1.10f   Develop mutually agreed-on intervention goals and objectives

Instructions:

A.   After formulating an innovative idea, mustering support from others, and identifying assets, it is time to specify your goals, objectives, and action steps in the IMAGINE macro change process. A *goal* is the end toward which effort is directed. Goals give you direction, but primary goals are usually so broadly stated that it is virtually impossible to specify how they will be achieved. For example, you might want to improve conditions in the Family Planning Center where you work. In order to accomplish this, you must break down that primary goal into a series of objectives. *Objectives* are smaller, behaviorally specific subgoals that serve as stepping stones on the way to accomplishing the primary goal. *Action steps* are tasks one must complete (in correct order and within the designated time frame) to achieve the desired objective—which, in turn, is designed to achieve your primary goal. The formula for creating an action step is to specify who will do what by when: *"Who"* is the individual that will accomplish the task; *"what"* is the task(s) assigned to that individual; and *"when"* sets a time limit so the task is not delayed or forgotten

B.   Read the following case scenarios, and identify the initial goals that would lead to the desired ends. Use the **who** will do **what** by **when** formula. Then list some objectives or subgoals that would help in achieving the larger goal. (Note that an arbitrary number of four goals are cited for each case vignette. You are free to establish more or fewer goals as you see fit. You also may establish any number of objectives and action steps to achieve each goal)

Vignette #1: Horace, a state parole agent, is a member of a Task Force to Curb Substance Abuse in his community.[1] He attends the first of a series of meetings aimed at facilitating a range of educational, prevention, and treatment programs to obliterate substance abuse among youth, especially delinquents. Other members include Bainbridge, a local judge; Uzzia, a lawyer working for the county to represent juveniles accused of felonies; and Wahkuna, a retired social worker who was an alcohol and other drug abuse counselor. They decide they need more information to determine the extent of the problem: How prevalent *is* drug abuse in this area? What prevention tactics are currently in use? What treatment facilities (type and quantity) are now in place? What diagnosis and assessment mechanisms would be appropriate? What treatment approaches are likely to be most effective?

Goal:

       Objectives:

         Action Steps:

---

[1] A task force is "a temporary group, usually within an organization, brought together to achieve some previously specified function or goal" (Barker, 2003, p. 430).

Goal:

    Objectives:

       Action Steps:

Goal:

    Objectives:

       Action Steps:

Goal:

    Objectives:

       Action Steps:

Vignette #2:   Marelda is a social worker at a homeless shelter in a large northeastern city. Facilities are simply inadequate to provide the necessary resources—including food, clothing, and shelter—for hundreds of homeless families. Suddenly Marelda has a brilliant idea. Why not make arrangements with the dozens—perhaps hundreds—of fast-food restaurants in the area to collect their unused food and distribute it to people in need? At the end of a day, remaining food is simply thrown out and goes to waste. Marelda begins to consider what support from friends and colleagues she might elicit, and how she might go about contacting fast-food restaurants and persuading them to support her cause.

Goal:

    Objectives:

       Action Steps:

Goal:

    Objectives:

        Action Steps:

Goal:

    Objectives:

        Action Steps:

Goal:

    Objectives:

        Action Steps:

Vignette #3:[2] Brian is a hospice social worker. The hospice movement rests on a philosophy of caring and an array of programs, services, and settings for people with terminal illness. Hospice services are usually offered in nonhospital facilities with homelike atmospheres where families, friends, and the significant other can be with the dying person (Barker, 1995, p. 171).

    Brian sees increasing numbers of gay patients entering the facility. He is aware of the special "issues of stigma, homophobia, and the cumulative effects of stress" experienced by gay people along with the devastating effects of their terminal illness (Dworkin & Kaufer, 1995, p. 41). He considers two possibilities. First, can he initiate support groups for patients, their families, and their partners? Second, to what extent are other hospice staff aware of the special issues facing gay people? Could the agency initiate in-service training to address this potential need? Brian thinks the hospice director would probably be very supportive of these his ideas—*if* Brian can figure out just how to implement them.

---

[2] This vignette is based on an account in J. Dworkin & D. Kaufer, "Social Services and Bereavement in the Lesbian and Gay Community," Vol. 2, No. 3/4, 1995, pp. 41-60.

Goal:

Objectives:

Action Steps:

Goal:

Objectives:

Action Steps:

Goal:

Objectives:

Action Steps:

Goal:

Objectives:

Action Steps:

95

Competencies/Practice Behaviors Exercise 6.5
Applying IMAGINE to Agency Policy Change

Focus Competencies or Practice Behaviors:
- EP 2.1.8a   Analyze, formulate, and advocate for policies that advance social well-being
- EP 2.1.8b   Collaborate with colleagues and clients for effective policy action

Instructions:

A.   Review the content on the IMAGINE process

B.   Apply IMAGINE to the following case example by responding to the questions that appear below.[3]

> Hsi-ping is a worker for the Comeasyouare County Department of Human Services. She and most other staff disagree with many policies initiated by Marcus, the agency director. Workers commonly refer to Marcus as Mr. Scrooge. They frequently question his decisions, which they believe are based on financial variables rather than clients' welfare.
>
> The latest problem is Marcus's decision to stop sending letters to clients without telephones. These letters announce that a particular worker will visit a client's home at a designated time. If that time is inconvenient, the client is asked to contact the worker to reschedule the visit. The letter then adds that the worker is looking forward to talking with the client. These letters have traditionally been sent out far enough in advance to allow clients to accommodate their own schedules or let the worker know beforehand that the time is inconvenient. Apparently, Marcus and his Chief Financial Manager, Millicent (often referred to as Ms. Scrooge), have figured out these letters cost the agency about five dollars apiece to send—including worker time, secretarial time, paper, postage, and any other agency efforts expended. Hsi-ping thinks Millicent read the five-dollar figure somewhere in a financial magazine and magically transformed it into a fact. She has a number of problems with the policy even if the figure is accurate.
>
> - First, it ignores clients' right to privacy, respect, and dignity. Dropping in on people unannounced is inconsiderate and simply rude.
> - Second, it violates clients' right to self-determination because it does not allow them any input in setting meeting times.
> - Third, it complicates both workers' and clients' lives. There is no guarantee that workers will arrive at convenient times for clients or that clients will even be at home.
>
> Hsi-Ping thinks about who might agree with her that this policy is unacceptable. She knows other staff in her own unit agree with her, but many of them are fairly new and would probably be hesitant to speak up. Hsi-Ping's supervisor Sphinctera follows regulations to the letter—even to the comma—without question. Nevertheless, Hsi-Ping likes Sphinctera, so she decides to share her feelings about the problem and see what reaction she gets.
>
> Much to Hsi-Ping's amazement, Sphinctera is very supportive of Hsi-Ping's position. Apparently, Sphinctera is tired of the agency's many policy changes and has difficulty keeping up with them. This no-letter policy is just too much. Sphinctera even comes up with an idea. Why not send out postcards announcing home visits? The cards could be preprinted for a nominal cost, workers could then address them, fill in the proposed visiting time, sign them, and send them out themselves.

---

[3] The idea and some details presented in this case example are taken from "The Appointment Letters," by G. H. Hull, Jr. In R. F. Rivas & G. H. Hull, Jr., *Case Studies in Generalist Practice* (Pacific Grove, CA: Brooks/Cole, 1996, pp. 150-53.)

It's a fine compromise—but Sphinctera hesitates to make waves and wants more information and more support before she will propose her idea to Marcus. Hsi-Ping volunteers to talk to her other colleagues in the unit, and verifies that they generally agree with her. One worker, Ruana, emphasizes her relief that someone else is addressing the problem. She tells Hsi-Ping about a home visit she made the day before, an unannounced visit because of the no-letter policy. It took her about an hour to get to the client's home and back. Since the client wasn't there, Ruana's time was wasted—at a cost to the agency of about $11 in salary for Ruana's wasted time and about $12 in mileage reimbursement. Even if Millicent and Marcus are correct that letters cost the agency $5, Ruana's useless trip cost $23, so the agency lost $18 under the new procedure. Imagine multiplying this by the hundreds of home visits workers regularly make.

Hsi-Ping reports her findings to Sphinctera. Together they decide to address the issue with Marcus. Sphinctera suggests doing so at one of the agency's regular staff meetings when staff are encouraged to voice their ideas and concerns (whether or not administrators are paying attention). She encourages Hsi-Ping to raise the issue because it was originally Hsi-Ping's idea. Hsi-Ping thinks Sphinctera is really afraid to initiate it herself, but she agrees to do the talking and thanks Sphinctera for her support. At the next staff meeting, Hsi-Ping expresses her concern about the no-letter policy. She takes a deep breath and is careful to speak with little emotion and no hostility. She presents the financial facts that support her proposal and emphasizes that she shares Marcus's concerns about the agency's finances. She then offers her suggestion and its rationale, adding that sending postcards was really Sphinctera's idea. Hsi-Ping adds that the postcards would not violate clients' confidentiality or privacy rights because they would carry no identifying information.

When she finishes, the eighty staff members in the room are dead silent for a few painful moments that seem like an eternity. Finally, six hands shoot up at once. One after another, staff support the idea. Hsi-Ping watches Marcus for some reaction. He looks straight ahead, says nothing, and pulls at his chin in his usual thoughtful gesture. Finally, he says, "You know, I think you just might have something here. Let's give it a try."

Hsi-Ping is overjoyed. She did it! She actually did it. She effected a substantive change in agency policy. Two days later Marcus sends a memo around the agency informing workers of the new change. Workers are generally pleased (although some old-timers still grumble that the letters were better). Marcus continues to seek new ways to cut costs—and, Hsi-Ping sometimes thinks, to make workers' lives miserable. However, the no-letter battle has been won and Hsi-Ping certainly is proud of that accomplishment.

Step 1: **IMAGINE**—Start with an Innovative *Idea*

A.   Summarize the problem presented above.

B.   Describe the innovative idea for a solution

C.   Explain the pros and cons of this idea

Step 2: IMAGINE—*Muster* Support and Formulate an Action System. Identify the following systems portrayed in the case scenario above

Macro client system

Change agent

Target system

Action system

Step 3: IMAGINE—Identify *Assets.* Identify the assets in Hsi-Ping's favor and explain why each is important

<u>Step 4: IMAGINE—Specify **Goals** and Objectives.</u> Identify the major goal Hsi-Ping wished to accomplish

      4a.   Identify specific objectives necessary for leading up to this goal. Use the *who* did *what* by *when* format

<u>Step 5: IMAGINE—**Implement** the Plan.</u> Evaluate and discuss the effectiveness of Hsi-Ping's implementation of her plan

<u>Step 6: IMAGINE—**Neutralize** Opposition.</u> Explain how Hsi-Ping determined who would assume which roles in the change effort

      6a.   Discuss the interpersonal dynamics determining who actually presented the issue and proposed recommendations

6b.   Explain how Hsi-Ping used persuasion to pursue her goal. What specific techniques did she use?

6c.   How might Hsi-Ping have used pressuring to attain her goal? What effects might pressuring have had?

Competencies/Practice Behaviors Exercise 6.6
Assessing an Organization's Cultural Competence

Focus Competencies or Practice Behaviors:
- EP 2.1.4   Engage diversity and difference in practice

Instructions:
A.   Review the material on culturally competent organizations
B.   Make an appointment with a worker or administrator at a social services agency in your area. (If necessary, you can conduct this interview by phone.) Solicit answers to the following five questions aimed at assessing an organization's cultural competence. Examples of questions you might use for further clarification are presented in brackets following each question

1.   *How responsible is the organization in responding effectively and efficiently to the needs of the culturally diverse people it serves* (Coggins & Fresquez, 2007; Hyde, 2003; Nybell & Gray, 2004)? [Does the agency have a good grasp of its clientele's cultural diversity? Must further research be performed to identify target client groups? To what extent does the agency create a "welcoming" climate for clients (Hyde, 2003, p. 51)?]

2.   *In what ways is the agency empowering its staff so that staff may, in turn, empower clients from diverse backgrounds* (Gutierrez & Lewis, 1999)? [To what extent do agency staff understand the needs, issues, and strengths of their diverse client population? Does the agency recruit, support, and retain leadership and direct service staff that reflect the client population's diversity? To what extent does the organization maintain values that reflect cultural competence and empowerment? To what degree does the agency provide multicultural training to enhance "knowledge about different racial and ethnic groups" and conduct "culturally sensitive client assessments" (Hyde, 2003, p. 53)?]

3.   *In what ways could services be administered differently in response to the needs of the agency's culturally diverse client population* (Coggins & Fresquez, 2007; Mason, 1994)? [Are services readily accessible to culturally diverse client groups? If not, how might the agency make such services more accessible? Is the communication between staff and clients as effective as it could be? Should workers offer services in different languages? Can agency personnel solicit information from significant community leaders or from clients to identify and pursue better service provision?]

4.   *What is the "organizational vision" with respect to the culturally diverse community* (Gutierrez & Lewis, 1999, p. 83)? [How might you best "envision the system as it should be and . . . identify ways of funding such a system" (Mason, 1994, p. 5)? How could you maximize the involvement of people who represent the diverse cultures your agency serves? How might you empower community residents? Can you and others helping you identify new potential resources for the community and the agency? Such resources might include "assisting with staff and board recruitment, encouraging . . . donations, identifying advocacy resources, and promoting parent or community education and support groups" (Mason, 1994, p. 5)]

5.   *How might you determine that the goal of cultural competence has been achieved* (Coggins & Fresquez, 2007; Mason, 1994)? [What specific objectives and action steps might you identify to provide clear proof that your purpose has been actualized? What task groups might you and the agency establish to review progress, refine recommendations, and keep efforts on target?]

Focus Competencies or Practice Behaviors:
- EP 2.1.3c Demonstrate effective oral and written communication in working with individuals, families, groups, organizations, communities, and colleagues

Instructions:
A. Review the content in the text on neutralizing opposition, including that on communicating with decision-makers, logical administrative reactions, phases of resistance, and collaborative and adversarial strategies
B. You will need to choose a classmate to complete this role play in which one will arbitrarily play the worker and the other the agency director described below

> ***WORKER ROLE:*** You are a case manager at an agency that provides diagnosis, treatment, and residential care for clients who have cognitive disabilities. The agency's policy for interdisciplinary treatment staffings is to include the designated client's MSW social worker (who provides therapy), psychologist, psychiatrist, physician, and nursing staff. Interdisciplinary treatment staffings are meetings held biannually for each client where staff involved with the client report the client's progress, discuss new treatment plans as necessary, and make specific recommendations for service provision.
>
> The problem is that you, as the client's case manager, are not invited to the staffings. You feel this is ridiculous because you are the one who works directly with clients on a daily or weekly basis and are charged with overseeing all service provision. The rationale for your exclusion is that you don't have a graduate degree. This makes no sense to you because nursing staff are included and they don't necessarily have graduate degrees either. You approach the agency director who is responsible for establishing much of agency policy and seeing that staff adhere to it.
>
> You have made an appointment to meet with the agency director. Use the suggestions for persuasion proposed in the box below and any others you can think of to persuade the director to amend policy to include you and other case managers in multidisciplinary treatment staffings.

Suggestions For Persuasion

1. Establish something you have in common with the agency director.
    (Suggestion: Concern for the clients' well-being and best interests.)

2. Share honest feelings.
    (Suggestions: Share your sincere desire to improve service provision. Empathize with the agency director's position as agency policy is not all that easy to change.)

3. Educate the decision-makers.
    (Suggestions: Elaborate on your role as case manager—without being condescending. Inform the director of the extra time it takes for you and other staff to communicate about treatment plans because you can't attend treatment staffings.)

4. Discuss options.
    (Suggestion: Discuss the potential advantages and disadvantages of your proposed plan.)

---

5. Ask if a trial or partial policy change is possible.
   (Suggestion: Is it possible to include the case manager in staffings for a temporary period of time on a trial basis?)

6. Suggest that a committee be formed to discuss and consider the proposed plan.

7. Creatively identify how spending more time with other team members during staffings could develop communication channels and become familiar with the issues from both sides.

8. Appeal to the agency director's sense of fairness, ethics, and right and wrong.
   (Suggestion: What is the most ethical approach to service provision for clients?)

9. Develop a rational argument to support your proposed plan.

10. Specify to the agency director what the negative consequences of the identified problem might be.
    (Suggestion: How will ignoring the problem result in costs to the director, the client, and the agency.)

AGENCY DIRECTOR: You are very busy overseeing numerous aspects of agency functioning. You are plagued by budget cuts, pressure from regulatory agencies to comply with codes, and various staffing problems. (For example, a former employee is suing the agency for sexual harassment by a psychologist who supervised her.)

You are very busy and have little time to waste on complaints or whining. You have agreed to see the case manager because you feel it is your responsibility to be in touch with your staff's issues. You understand this issue is something about a policy change, but you don't know much more than that. In general, you hate policy changes. The process is time-consuming and there are usually unanticipated results, many of which are negative.

C. After the role play, address the following questions
   1. What happened during the role play?

   2. Which suggestions for persuasion worked and which didn't? Explain.

3.   What other suggestions do you have for successful persuasion?

4.   From this experience, what have you learned about the persuasion process?

105

Chapter 6 Competencies or Practice Behaviors Exercises Assessment:

Name: _____ **Date:** _____
Supervisor's Name: _____

Focus Competencies/Practice Behaviors:
- EP 2.1.3c   Demonstrate effective oral and written communication in working with individuals, families, groups, organizations, communities, and colleagues
- EP 2.1.7a   Utilize conceptual frameworks to guide the processes of assessment, intervention, and evaluation
- EP 2.1.8a   Analyze, formulate, and advocate for policies that advance social well-being
- EP 2.1.8b   Collaborate with colleagues and clients for effective policy action
- EP 2.1.10e   Assess client strengths and limitations
- EP 2.1.10f   Develop mutually agreed-on intervention goals and objectives

Instructions:

A.   Evaluate your work or your partner's work in the Focus Competencies/Practice Behaviors by completing the Competencies/Practice Behaviors Assessment form below

B.   What other Competencies/Practice Behaviors did you use to complete these Exercises? Be sure to record them in your assessments

1.	I have attained this competency/practice behavior (in the range of 81 to 100%)
2.	I have largely attained this competency/practice behavior (in the range of 61 to 80%)
3.	I have partially attained this competency/practice behavior (in the range of 41 to 60%)
4.	I have made a little progress in attaining this competency/practice behavior (in the range of 21 to 40%)
5.	I have made almost no progress in attaining this competency/practice behavior (in the range of 0 to 20%)

EPAS 2008 Core Competencies & Core Practice Behaviors	Student Self Assessment						Evaluator Feedback
Student and Evaluator Assessment Scale and Comments	0	1	2	3	4	5	Agree/Disagree/Comments
EP 2.1.1 Identify as a Professional Social Worker and Conduct Oneself Accordingly							
a. Advocate for client access to the services of social work							
b. Practice personal reflection and self-correction to assure continual professional development							
c. Attend to professional roles and boundaries							
d. Demonstrate professional demeanor in behavior, appearance, and communication							
e. Engage in career-long learning							
f. Use supervision and consultation							
EP 2.1.2 Apply Social Work Ethical Principles to Guide Professional Practice							
a. Recognize and manage personal values in a way that allows professional values to guide practice							
b. Make ethical decisions by applying NASW Code of Ethics and, as applicable, of the IFSW/IASSW Ethics in Social Work, Statement of Principles							

c.	Tolerate ambiguity in resolving ethical conflicts						
d.	Apply strategies of ethical reasoning to arrive at principled decisions						
EP 2.1.3 Apply Critical Thinking to Inform and Communicate Professional Judgments							
a.	Distinguish, appraise, and integrate multiple sources of knowledge, including research-based knowledge and practice wisdom						
b.	Analyze models of assessment, prevention, intervention, and evaluation						
c.	Demonstrate effective oral and written communication in working with individuals, families, groups, organizations, communities, and colleagues						
EP 2.1.4 Engage Diversity and Difference in Practice							
a.	Recognize the extent to which a culture's structures and values may oppress, marginalize, alienate, or create or enhance privilege and power						
b.	Gain sufficient self-awareness to eliminate the influence of personal biases and values in working with diverse groups						
c.	Recognize and communicate their understanding of the importance of difference in shaping life experiences						
d.	View themselves as learners and engage those with whom they work as informants						
EP 2.1.5 Advance Human Rights and Social and Economic Justice							
a.	Understand forms and mechanisms of oppression and discrimination						
b.	Advocate for human rights and social and economic justice						
c.	Engage in practices that advance social and economic justice						
EP 2.1.6 Engage in Research-Informed Practice and Practice-Informed Research							
a.	Use practice experience to inform scientific inquiry						
b.	Use research evidence to inform practice						
EP 2.1.7 Apply Knowledge of Human Behavior and the Social Environment							
a.	Utilize conceptual frameworks to guide the processes of assessment, intervention, and evaluation						
b.	Critique and apply knowledge to understand person and environment						
EP 2.1.8 Engage in Policy Practice to Advance Social and Economic Well-Being and to Deliver Effective Social Work Services							
a.	Analyze, formulate, and advocate for policies that advance social well-being						
b.	Collaborate with colleagues and clients for effective policy action						
EP 2.1.9 Respond to Contexts that Shape Practice							
a.	Continuously discover, appraise, and attend to changing locales, populations, scientific and technological developments, and emerging societal trends to provide relevant services						

b.	Provide leadership in promoting sustainable changes in service delivery and practice to improve the quality of social services						
EP 2.1.10 Engage, Assess, Intervene, and Evaluate with Individuals, Families, Groups, Organizations and Communities							
a.	Substantively and affectively prepare for action with individuals, families, groups, organizations, and communities						
b.	Use empathy and other interpersonal skills						
c.	Develop a mutually agreed-on focus of work and desired outcomes						
d.	Collect, organize, and interpret client data						
e.	Assess client strengths and limitations						
f.	Develop mutually agreed-on intervention goals and objectives						
g.	Select appropriate intervention strategies						
h.	Initiate actions to achieve organizational goals						
i.	Implement prevention interventions that enhance client capacities						
j.	Help clients resolve problems						
k.	Negotiate, mediate, and advocate for clients						
l.	Facilitate transitions and endings						
m.	Critically analyze, monitor, and evaluate interventions						

Competencies/Practice Behaviors Exercise 7.1
Assessing an Organization's Cultural Competence

Focus Competencies or Practice Behaviors:
- EP 2.1.10a   Substantively and affectively prepare for action with individuals, families, groups, organizations, and communities
- EP 2.1.10c   Develop a mutually agreed-on focus of work and desired outcomes
- EP 2.1.10e   Assess client strengths and limitations

Instructions:
A.   Review the material in the text on using the IMAGINE process to develop a program
B.   Read each vignette below. Respond to the subsequent instructions and questions concerning the application of the first three steps of the IMAGINE process to program development as it might apply to the vignette

> **VIGNETTE A:**   You are a social worker in a Veteran's Administration (VA) Hospital in East LA.   The VA, a federal organization initially established in 1920, provides a wide range of services to people who have served in the military in order to enhance their overall health and welfare; services include those directed at physical and mental illness, vocational training, financial assistance, and a host of others (Barker, 1999).   Specifically, you work in a unit that provides short-term housing and alcohol and other drug (AODA) treatment for homeless veterans. The problem is that you're finding that more and more of your clients come to you and tell you they simply can't find any full-time jobs, even for minimum wage. You find yourself thinking more and more frequently to yourself, "Even a full-time minimum wage job is pretty much a bummer in terms of taking care of yourself."
>
> The issue you really feel boils down to adequate job training. Why can't the VA provide educational and vocational training, or else finance its purchase through some other agency? You have looked and looked for resources for your clients. They need to get back on their feet again. They need work that is relatively permanent, provides an adequate standard of living, and enhances their self esteem. What you and your clients really need is a job-training program with a strong educational component. But there isn't one. Now what?

1.   **IMAGINE Step 1:** Develop an innovative **idea.**

   Propose and describe a program that you feel would meet clients' identified needs.

2.   IMAGINE Step 2: **Muster** support.

Who might be appropriate action system members from the agency and community in this situation? Explain why.

3.   IMAGINE Step 3: Identify **assets.**

   a.   What variables might exist that could support your change efforts?

   b.   Who else in the agency might be called upon for support (other than action system members)?

   c.   How might you work to enhance your own power?

   d.   What potential funding sources might you pursue?

Vignette B: You are an intake worker for the Sheboygan County Department of Social Services. The county is primarily rural with a smattering of small towns. Your primary job is to take calls from people requesting services, gather initial information about them and their problems, provide them with some information about county services, and make appropriate referrals to the agencies whose services they need.

You are alarmed at the growing number of calls concerning older adults having difficulty maintaining themselves in their own homes. Most are calls from neighbors, relatives, or the older adults themselves. Examples of concerns include: worries about falling and remaining stranded for days; forgetfulness (such as leaving the stove's gas burner on); lack of transportation to get to a critical doctor's appointment; difficulties in understanding complicated health insurance and Medicare reimbursements; and depression due to loneliness and isolation.

After you receive such calls, you typically refer the callers to the Department's Protective Services for Older Adults unit. However, you know all the unit can usually do is make an assessment home visit and either refer the client to a local nursing home or terminate the case. That's depressing. Many of these people just need company and supportive help to maintain their independent living conditions. You have heard of such programs in other parts of the state. It would be great to have a program through which staff could visit similar clients, help them with daily tasks, transport them to recreational activities, and generally provide friendly support. Such a program would help these older adults remain in their own homes. Can you initiate such a program?

IMAGINE Step 1: Develop an innovative **idea.**

Propose and describe a program that you feel would meet clients' identified needs.

IMAGINE Step 2: **Muster** support.

Who in your agency and/or community might be appropriate action system members for this macro change? Explain why.

IMAGINE Step 3: Identify **assets.**

      a.   What variables might exist that could support your change efforts?

      b.   Who else in the agency might be called upon for support (other than action system members)?

      c.   How might you work to enhance your own power?

      d.   What potential funding sources might you pursue?

Vignette C: You are a state probation officer. You notice a significant increase in your caseload (that is, the clients assigned to you) of men repeatedly committing acts that in your state are considered misdemeanors. A misdemeanor is a minor crime—less serious than a felony—that generally results in incarceration of less than six months (Barker, 1991, p. 146). These men, for example, are speeding while driving under the influence, shoplifting items such as CDs, and even urinating when driving a car. (This last incident actually happened, although it's hard to picture.) As their probation officer, you see these "dumb" things getting them several-hundred-dollar fines and several-month jail sentences. You think this is senseless. There must be a better way to deal with this problem and to make these men more responsible for their behavior.

At a conference you hear about a "deferred prosecution" approach in an adjoining state. This program provides men arrested for such misdemeanors with alternatives to fines and jail terms. They can opt to participate in a 12-week group run by two social workers. Group sessions focus on enhancing self-esteem, raising self-awareness, improving decision-making skills, developing better communication skills, and encouraging the analysis of responsible versus irresponsible behavior. The program was initially funded by a grant (often referred to as "soft money," meaning temporary and limited funding), but it was so successful that the state now implements and pays for it in several designated counties with "hard money." ("Hard money" means relatively permanent funding that becomes part of an organization's regular annual budget.)

Men who participated in the program had a significantly reduced recidivism rate. *Recidivism rates* in this context refer to the proportion of offenders who continue to commit misdemeanors. A recidivism rate of 25 percent, then, would mean that of 100 men, 25 committed additional misdemeanors and 75 did not.

You think, "What a wonderful idea!" You begin to investigate how you can initiate such a program in your agency.

IMAGINE Step 1: Develop an innovative *idea*.

Propose and describe a program that you feel would meet clients' identified needs.

IMAGINE Step 2: *Muster* support.

Who in your agency and/or community might be appropriate action system members for this macro change? Explain why.

IMAGINE Step 3: Identify *assets.*

    a.   What variables might exist that could support your change efforts?

    b.   Who else in the agency might be called upon for support (other than action system members)?

    c.   How might you work to enhance your own power?

    d.   What potential funding sources might you pursue?

Competencies/Practice Behaviors Exercise 7.2
Creative Projects

Focus Competencies or Practice Behaviors:
- EP 2.1.10g   Select appropriate intervention strategies

Instructions:
A.   Review content on examples of projects in macro practice
B.   Read the following case vignettes and respond to the questions about potential project implementation

Vignette #1: Manuela is a Protective Services Worker who helps "legal authorities with investigations to determine if children are in need of such services, help[s] children get services when needed," and provides family counseling (Barker, 1995, p. 56). Most of her clients are very poor, and since Thanksgiving is approaching, Manuela worries that many of them will be unable to have much food at all, let alone a grand turkey celebration.

What types of projects could Manuela initiate? Specifically, how might she go about doing so?

Vignette #2: Dougal is a counselor at a large urban YMCA. He organizes and runs recreational and educational programs for youth, functions as a positive role model, and provides informal counseling. Recently, he learned that the county social services agency had contracted with an expert on gang intervention to run a four-day in-service program for its staff. Dougal thinks it would be extremely helpful to the staff at the "Y" if they could somehow participate in such a program.

What sort of project might Dougal initiate to get in-service training for the "Y" staff? Specifically, how might he go about doing so?

Vignette #3: Jarita works at a Planned Parenthood organization where she does contraception and pregnancy counseling. She is also invited to give educational presentations to large groups of people. She finds that over the years her job has significantly changed: Whereas she once dealt primarily with contraception counseling, she now spends more time providing sex education, especially with respect to AIDS. Along with the changes in her job, many other changes have occurred in the agency over the past ten years. For one thing, it is much larger than it was when Jarita began working there. More restrictive state legislation has affected the referral process for abortions. Much more emphasis is now placed on sex education. Jarita observes that the agency policy manual has simply not kept up with the agency's progress and development. Even some personnel policies such as insurance coverage have changed significantly over time. Simply put, the policy manual is colossally out of date.

What sort of project might Jarita pursue in dealing with this concern? Specifically, how might she go about doing so?

Competencies/Practice Behaviors Exercise 7.3
Role Play PERT charts

Focus Competencies or Practice Behaviors:
- EP 2.1.10a   Substantively and affectively prepare for action with individuals, families, groups, organizations, and communities
- EP 2.1.10b   Use empathy and other interpersonal skills
- EP 2.1.10c   Develop a mutually agreed-on focus of work and desired outcomes

Instructions:

A.   Review the content on PERT charts

B.   Review the following description regarding how the role play will proceed

C.   The role play requires five characters: two unit counselors (change agents); the school's principal; a social work therapist; and the unit counselors' supervisor. In order to reflect real professional life, each character has a professional and individual personality, and a personal agenda. The practice setting is Getalife, a residential treatment center for male adolescents with severe behavioral and emotional problems

D.   Remaining students should observe the role play and record their impressions on the Feedback Form included here. Role players should not record observations on Feedback Forms because that distracts from their role enactment

E.   Each role player should then read out loud his or her respective lines

F.   Review the organizational chart included below to understand the agency's chain of command. (Note that in the organizational chart the positions of people involved in the role play are highlighted in boldface italics)

G.   Begin the role play and allow it to continue for approximately 20 minutes. One person should be responsible for halting the role play after the time has elapsed

H.   After the role play is halted, the group should discuss critical points, constructive techniques, and suggestions for improvement concerning what occurred. Use the feedback forms to aid in discussion

---

Unit Counselor #1: Your job is to supervise daily living and recreational activities for Getalife's residents, to implement individual residents' behavioral programming, to keep records, and to participate in the residents' group counseling sessions. You also periodically attend staffings where individual case plans are established, implemented, and updated. You work in the Box Elder Unit which includes fourteen boys ages 13 to 15. You have worked for the agency for two years, like your job, and feel you can make valuable contributions to residents' well-being. You are especially concerned about residents' need for sex education. Many—perhaps most—of the center's residents have been sexually active. You know this from talking with residents, reading records, and attending treatment conferences where such information is shared and addressed.

116

You can't think of anyone in the residential center—including child-care workers, teachers, social workers, or administrators—who has an expertise in this area. You set up a meeting with the head child-care worker (your direct supervisor), the residential unit's social work therapist, and the school's principal to establish a plan. You have already explained to them your general idea so that they will have time to think about the issues prior to the meeting. You have discussed your ideas in greater depth with Unit Counselor #2 who seems to agree strongly with you and is willing to help you conduct the meeting. Together you hope to convince this group of the usefulness of your plan. You intend to establish a PERT chart for how to go about setting up a series of sex education sessions for your unit's residents.

You feel that sex education is tremendously important. You have a 14-year-old sister who is pregnant, and that adds to the significance of this issue for you. You are happy that Worker #2 agrees with you and is willing to help you pursue a sex education program for the Box Elder Unit. However, you believe that you are more committed to the issue than Worker #2, and you would like to apply some pressure on Worker #2 to take on more responsibility for planning and implementing the program.

Unit Counselor #2: You work in the Box Elder Unit with Worker #1 who has talked to you about the sex education proposal. You think that sex education is a very important need for the boys in the Box Elder Unit, but you are pretty busy with your job and you are going to school part-time. You'd like to get the sex education program going, but you don't have much extra time for planning or implementation. You like and respect Worker #1, and you realize that Worker #1 is extremely committed to the issue. It seems logical to you that Worker #1 should take on the most responsibility for planning and implementation. You are willing to expend substantial energy to get a PERT plan in place, but you would then like to minimize your involvement in the plan's implementation.

The Center's School Principal: You supervise six special education teachers and their six respective assistants in Getalife's on-grounds school. You have been with the center for three years, and you believe that anything related to education comes under the school's responsibility. Right now, the school is pressed for resources, and you consider sex education a frill that the school can't afford to address. What's more, in your opinion none of the current educational staff has any expertise in this area, and you wonder whether they would feel comfortable teaching about sexuality. All in all, you resent having to attend this meeting. You wish that the two workers would just drop the subject and mind their own business. You also don't much like the Box Elder Unit's social work therapist. You see the therapist as an ineffective employee in a cushy job. You believe that a good education will offer the adolescent residents more hope for their futures than is likely to come from talking about their feelings with some social worker in hocus-pocus, psychobabble therapy. In short, you have very little confidence that the social workers can accomplish much.

You don't plan to support this "sex plan," and you're coming up with a list of reasons that it's a dumb idea. If in the end the group decides to implement it anyway, you definitely want the programming to be provided by an expert from outside the agency. On this point you do not intend to budge.

The Box Elder Unit's Social Work Therapist: You are an MSW charged with providing the adolescents in your unit with one hour of individual therapy and two hours of group therapy each week, in addition to any family counseling that is deemed necessary. You also assist staff in developing behavioral programming, coordinate residents' individual plans through periodic staffings, write staffing summary reports, coordinate staff activity in implementing treatment recommendations, and monitor residents' progress. You have been with the agency for almost six months.

You are a relatively new "gung-ho" social worker, anxious to do your job and do it well. You have finally been able to get your bearings after six months of struggling to figure out how the agency operates and what you're doing with your clients. You have had some difficulty working with both the school principal and the head child-care supervisor. Both seem to resent any suggestions you make for treatment and your efforts to implement treatment plans in the unit and in the school. Without consistency and follow-through, it's hard to get your clients' behavioral programming to work. The principal is especially difficult to work with and very protective of school turf. The head child-care supervisor is more easy-going but appears to "know everything." You feel the supervisor treats you rather condescendingly and doesn't always come through after promising that something will get done. You think the supervisor is pretty passive-aggressive.

You really like the idea of implementing the sexuality programming. You took a sexuality course in college and have had some subsequent training, so with some brushing up on the content you think you could present a really good program. You also feel it would enhance your relationship with your clients.

The Unit Counselors' Supervisor: You supervise all the counselors (child-care) for the residential center's six units—a total of 58 full-time and part-time staff. You are responsible for scheduling their shifts, supervising their work, and arranging for training to meet ongoing treatment needs. You have an associate's degree from a local community college and have been in your current position for the past 17 years.

Since you have been at the agency an awfully long time, you believe that you really know what's going on. These young whippersnappers on the staff come and go, but you maintain continuity for ongoing treatment and care. You also feel that you're pretty much "a natural" with the kids. You don't need a lot of fancy degrees to work effectively with the residents and develop caring and consistent programs for them. You feel you've helped many, many young people get their acts together. You haven't as yet developed confidence in the social work therapist's ability to work effectively with the residents. The social worker seems to you to have promise, but still needs more experience. You think the school principal is rather cocky, but then you've seen half a dozen principals come and go. You're pretty easy-going and are willing to work with the principal's "eccentric" behaviors and needs.

You attend this meeting out of respect for your two Potawatomi Unit Counselors. You like to encourage your staff to develop new ideas. You also like to present opportunities for them to do so. You feel that it would be best for the agency if some in-house staff did the programming. After all, this idea is basically a fad or frill. Why should the agency expend its scarce resources to pay some expert to come in? Why not have some volunteer staff do the sex ed programming and, essentially, get it over with?

PERT Role Play Organizational

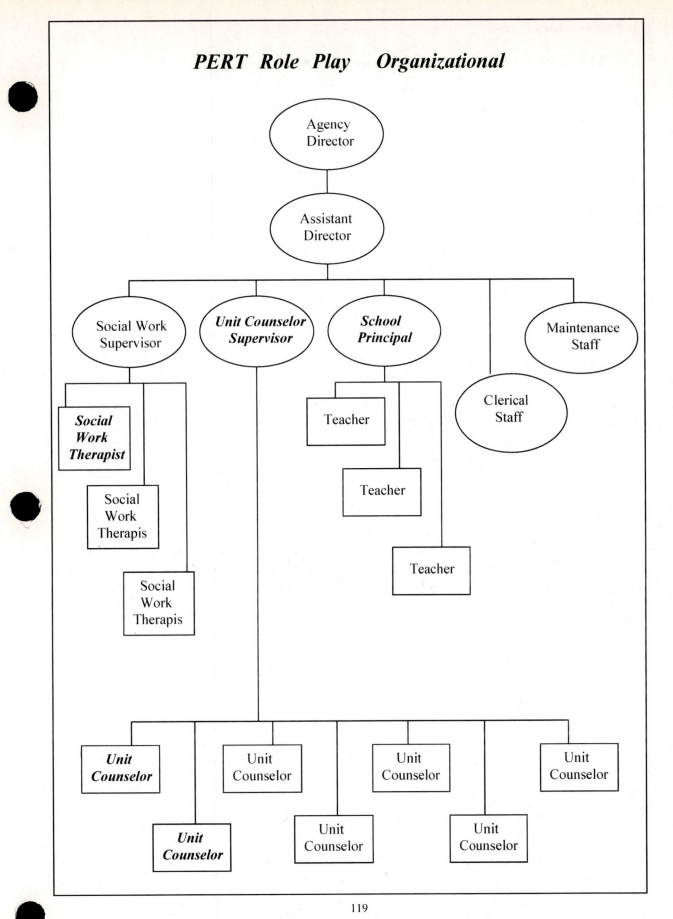

Role Play Feedback Form

1. What were the critical points or major issues addressed in the role play?

2. What especially helpful techniques and approaches were used? Please be specific.

3. What specific suggestions for improvement can you make? For example, how could issues have been addressed more effectively? What alternative responses might have solicited more information or cooperation? Please be specific.

Chapter 7 Competencies or Practice Behaviors Exercises Assessment:

Name: _____ **Date:** _____

Supervisor's Name: _____

Focus Competencies/Practice Behaviors:
- EP 2.1.10a   Substantively and affectively prepare for action with individuals, families, groups, organizations, and communities
- EP 2.1.10b   Use empathy and other interpersonal skills
- EP 2.1.10c   Develop a mutually agreed-on focus of work and desired outcomes
- EP 2.1.10e   Assess client strengths and limitations
- EP 2.1.10g   Select appropriate intervention strategies

Instructions:
A.   Evaluate your work or your partner's work in the Focus Competencies/Practice Behaviors by completing the Competencies/Practice Behaviors Assessment form below
B.   What other Competencies/Practice Behaviors did you use to complete these Exercises? Be sure to record them in your assessments

1.	I have attained this competency/practice behavior (in the range of 81 to 100%)
2.	I have largely attained this competency/practice behavior (in the range of 61 to 80%)
3.	I have partially attained this competency/practice behavior (in the range of 41 to 60%)
4.	I have made a little progress in attaining this competency/practice behavior (in the range of 21 to 40%)
5.	I have made almost no progress in attaining this competency/practice behavior (in the range of 0 to 20%)

EPAS 2008 Core Competencies & Core Practice Behaviors	Student Self Assessment						Evaluator Feedback
Student and Evaluator Assessment Scale and Comments	0	1	2	3	4	5	Agree/Disagree/Comments
EP 2.1.1 Identify as a Professional Social Worker and Conduct Oneself Accordingly							
a. Advocate for client access to the services of social work							
b. Practice personal reflection and self-correction to assure continual professional development							
c. Attend to professional roles and boundaries							
d. Demonstrate professional demeanor in behavior, appearance, and communication							
e. Engage in career-long learning							
f. Use supervision and consultation							
EP 2.1.2 Apply Social Work Ethical Principles to Guide Professional Practice							
a. Recognize and manage personal values in a way that allows professional values to guide practice							
b. Make ethical decisions by applying NASW Code of Ethics and, as applicable, of the IFSW/IASSW Ethics in Social Work, Statement of Principles							
c. Tolerate ambiguity in resolving ethical conflicts							
d. Apply strategies of ethical reasoning to arrive at principled decisions							

121

EP 2.1.3 Apply Critical Thinking to Inform and Communicate Professional Judgments							
a.	Distinguish, appraise, and integrate multiple sources of knowledge, including research-based knowledge and practice wisdom						
b.	Analyze models of assessment, prevention, intervention, and evaluation						
c.	Demonstrate effective oral and written communication in working with individuals, families, groups, organizations, communities, and colleagues						
EP 2.1.4 Engage Diversity and Difference in Practice							
a.	Recognize the extent to which a culture's structures and values may oppress, marginalize, alienate, or create or enhance privilege and power						
b.	Gain sufficient self-awareness to eliminate the influence of personal biases and values in working with diverse groups						
c.	Recognize and communicate their understanding of the importance of difference in shaping life experiences						
d.	View themselves as learners and engage those with whom they work as informants						
EP 2.1.5 Advance Human Rights and Social and Economic Justice							
a.	Understand forms and mechanisms of oppression and discrimination						
b.	Advocate for human rights and social and economic justice						
c.	Engage in practices that advance social and economic justice						
EP 2.1.6 Engage in Research-Informed Practice and Practice-Informed Research							
a.	Use practice experience to inform scientific inquiry						
b.	Use research evidence to inform practice						
EP 2.1.7 Apply Knowledge of Human Behavior and the Social Environment							
a.	Utilize conceptual frameworks to guide the processes of assessment, intervention, and evaluation						
b.	Critique and apply knowledge to understand person and environment						
EP 2.1.8 Engage in Policy Practice to Advance Social and Economic Well-Being and to Deliver Effective Social Work Services							
a.	Analyze, formulate, and advocate for policies that advance social well-being						
b.	Collaborate with colleagues and clients for effective policy action						
EP 2.1.9 Respond to Contexts that Shape Practice							
a.	Continuously discover, appraise, and attend to changing locales, populations, scientific and technological developments, and emerging societal trends to provide relevant services						
b.	Provide leadership in promoting sustainable changes in service delivery and practice to improve the quality of social services						

EP 2.1.10 Engage, Assess, Intervene, and Evaluate with Individuals, Families, Groups, Organizations and Communities						
a. Substantively and affectively prepare for action with individuals, families, groups, organizations, and communities						
b. Use empathy and other interpersonal skills						
c. Develop a mutually agreed-on focus of work and desired outcomes						
d. Collect, organize, and interpret client data						
e. Assess client strengths and limitations						
f. Develop mutually agreed-on intervention goals and objectives						
g. Select appropriate intervention strategies						
h. Initiate actions to achieve organizational goals						
i. Implement prevention interventions that enhance client capacities						
j. Help clients resolve problems						
k. Negotiate, mediate, and advocate for clients						
l. Facilitate transitions and endings						
m. Critically analyze, monitor, and evaluate interventions						

123

Competencies/Practice Behaviors Exercise 8.1
Nontraditional Communities

Focus Competencies or Practice Behaviors:

- EP 2.1.7a   Utilize conceptual frameworks to guide the processes of assessment, intervention, and evaluation
- EP 2.1.10   Engage, assess, intervene, and evaluate with individuals, families, groups, organizations, and communities

Instructions:

A.   List all the communities of which you are a member

B.   Place a checkmark in the appropriate column indicating whether it is a traditional or nontraditional community

Community	Traditional	Nontraditional

Competencies/Practice Behaviors Exercise 8.2
Assessing Community Effectiveness

Focus Competencies or Practice Behaviors:

- EP 2.1.7a   Utilize conceptual frameworks to guide the processes of assessment, intervention, and evaluation
- EP 2.1.10a   Substantively and affectively prepare for action with individuals, families, groups, organizations, and communities

Instructions:

A.   Look at your hometown and assess how well your community performed the functions expected of a community

B.   Suggest ways in which a less well-performed function could be enhanced

Competencies/Practice Behaviors Exercise 8.3
Identifying Systems

Focus Competencies or Practice Behaviors:
- EP 2.1.7a   Utilize conceptual frameworks to guide the processes of assessment, intervention, and evaluation
- EP 2.1.7b   Critique and apply knowledge to understand person and environment

Instructions:
A.   Read the following case illustration
B.   Identify client, action, change agent, and target systems within this community

Livermore is a small East Coast city with a big problem. Situated along a major interstate highway, it has become a haven for street gangs and drug dealers because it has only a small police force and is less able than the nearby large city of St. Trump to arrest and prosecute these criminals. Mary Mercado moved to Livermore to escape the violence and crime in St. Trump. As a hospital social worker, she knew first-hand the effects of violence. Worried that her new city is going to end up like her old one, Mary talks with a few of her friends who suggest that she bring her concerns to the attention of her city council representative. Mary meets with Paul Hernandez and together they ask the city council to fund a small task force.

The task force (composed of Mary, Paul, another city council member, the city attorney, a probation and parole officer [who is a social worker], and the police chief) prepares a report recommending that the city take seven steps to reduce or eliminate the drug and gang problem in Livermore.

Identify the following systems:

Client system

Action system

Change agent system

Target system

Competencies/Practice Behaviors Exercise 8.4
Which Theory Is Most Helpful?

Focus Competencies or Practice Behaviors:
- EP 2.1.7a   Utilize conceptual frameworks to guide the processes of assessment, intervention, and evaluation
- EP 2.1.7b   Critique and apply knowledge to understand person and environment

Instructions:

A.   Read each of the community situations listed in the box below

B.   Select which theory (ecological, human behavior, social systems, social structural, or organizational) best explains each particular community event

---

Which theory is most useful in understanding each of these community situations?

A.   The largest employer in a community goes out of business, throwing hundreds of people out of work.

   Theory:

   Explanation:

B.   A large community attempts to annex (take over) an adjacent smaller community.

   Theory:

   Explanation:

C.   The business sector in a community is deteriorating. Business owners are resisting community attempts to revitalize the downtown area and are failing to improve their own businesses.

   Theory:

   Explanation:

D. The city council has passed a resolution calling for the city building inspector and the police department to work together to target deteriorated buildings and fine landlords who fail to keep up their properties. This is the first attempt to get these two bodies working together.

Theory:

Explanation:

E. Maria Hatcher no longer calls the police when shots ring out in her neighborhood. After all, the police have been unable to stop the violence since it began three years ago.

Theory:

Explanation:

Competencies/Practice Behaviors Exercise 8.5
Role Play Designing a Model for Community Assessment

Focus Competencies or Practice Behaviors:
- EP 2.1.10d   Collect, organize, and interpret client data

Instructions:
A.   Your unit has been given the task of designing a community assessment model to be presented at the next Board meeting. This assessment is for the purpose of deciding whether to establish a youth center in the community.
B.   This is a brainstorming session to establish the specific categories for this assessment, as well as who to contact for data.
C.   One person will be in charge of keeping the minutes of this meeting, one person will be designated to write up the final Assessment Model. You all will need to critique the process as to what went right, what went wrong, and how you would have done things differently.
D.   Use the next page for your critique. Use separate paper for the minutes and the final Assessment Model.

Chapter 8 Competencies/Practice Behaviors Exercises Assessment:

Name: _____ **Date:** _____

Supervisor's Name: _____

Focus Competencies/Practice Behaviors:
- EP 2.1.7a   Utilize conceptual frameworks to guide the processes of assessment, intervention, and evaluation
- EP 2.1.7b   Critique and apply knowledge to understand person and environment
- EP 2.1.10   Engage, assess, intervene, and evaluate with individuals, families, groups, organizations, and communities
- EP 2.1.10a   Substantively and affectively prepare for action with individuals, families, groups, organizations, and communities
- EP 2.1.10d   Collect, organize, and interpret client data

Instructions:

A.   Evaluate your work or your partner's work in the Focus Competencies/Practice Behaviors by completing the Competencies/Practice Behaviors Assessment form below

B.   What other Competencies/Practice Behaviors did you use to complete these Exercises? Be sure to record them in your assessments

1.	I have attained this competency/practice behavior (in the range of 81 to 100%)
2.	I have largely attained this competency/practice behavior (in the range of 61 to 80%)
3.	I have partially attained this competency/practice behavior (in the range of 41 to 60%)
4.	I have made a little progress in attaining this competency/practice behavior (in the range of 21 to 40%)
5.	I have made almost no progress in attaining this competency/practice behavior (in the range of 0 to 20%)

Student and Evaluator Assessment Scale and Comments	0	1	2	3	4	5	Agree/Disagree/Comments
EP 2.1.1 Identify as a Professional Social Worker and Conduct Oneself Accordingly							
a. Advocate for client access to the services of social work							
b. Practice personal reflection and self-correction to assure continual professional development							
c. Attend to professional roles and boundaries							
d. Demonstrate professional demeanor in behavior, appearance, and communication							
e. Engage in career-long learning							
f. Use supervision and consultation							
EP 2.1.2 Apply Social Work Ethical Principles to Guide Professional Practice							
a. Recognize and manage personal values in a way that allows professional values to guide practice							
b. Make ethical decisions by applying NASW Code of Ethics and, as applicable, of the IFSW/IASSW Ethics in Social Work, Statement of Principles							
c. Tolerate ambiguity in resolving ethical conflicts							
d. Apply strategies of ethical reasoning to arrive at principled decisions							

129

EP 2.1.3 Apply Critical Thinking to Inform and Communicate Professional Judgments						
a.	Distinguish, appraise, and integrate multiple sources of knowledge, including research-based knowledge and practice wisdom					
b.	Analyze models of assessment, prevention, intervention, and evaluation					
c.	Demonstrate effective oral and written communication in working with individuals, families, groups, organizations, communities, and colleagues					
EP 2.1.4 Engage Diversity and Difference in Practice						
a.	Recognize the extent to which a culture's structures and values may oppress, marginalize, alienate, or create or enhance privilege and power					
b.	Gain sufficient self-awareness to eliminate the influence of personal biases and values in working with diverse groups					
c.	Recognize and communicate their understanding of the importance of difference in shaping life experiences					
d.	View themselves as learners and engage those with whom they work as informants					
EP 2.1.5 Advance Human Rights and Social and Economic Justice						
a.	Understand forms and mechanisms of oppression and discrimination					
b.	Advocate for human rights and social and economic justice					
c.	Engage in practices that advance social and economic justice					
EP 2.1.6 Engage in Research-Informed Practice and Practice-Informed Research						
a.	Use practice experience to inform scientific inquiry					
b.	Use research evidence to inform practice					
EP 2.1.7 Apply Knowledge of Human Behavior and the Social Environment						
a.	Utilize conceptual frameworks to guide the processes of assessment, intervention, and evaluation					
b.	Critique and apply knowledge to understand person and environment					
EP 2.1.8 Engage in Policy Practice to Advance Social and Economic Well-Being and to Deliver Effective Social Work Services						
a.	Analyze, formulate, and advocate for policies that advance social well-being					
b.	Collaborate with colleagues and clients for effective policy action					
EP 2.1.9 Respond to Contexts that Shape Practice						
a.	Continuously discover, appraise, and attend to changing locales, populations, scientific and technological developments, and emerging societal trends to provide relevant services					
b.	Provide leadership in promoting sustainable changes in service delivery and practice to improve the quality of social services					

EP 2.1.10 Engage, Assess, Intervene, and Evaluate with Individuals, Families, Groups, Organizations and Communities							
a.	Substantively and affectively prepare for action with individuals, families, groups, organizations, and communities						
b.	Use empathy and other interpersonal skills						
c.	Develop a mutually agreed-on focus of work and desired outcomes						
d.	Collect, organize, and interpret client data						
e.	Assess client strengths and limitations						
f.	Develop mutually agreed-on intervention goals and objectives						
g.	Select appropriate intervention strategies						
h.	Initiate actions to achieve organizational goals						
i.	Implement prevention interventions that enhance client capacities						
j.	Help clients resolve problems						
k.	Negotiate, mediate, and advocate for clients						
l.	Facilitate transitions and endings						
m.	Critically analyze, monitor, and evaluate interventions						

Competencies/Practice Behaviors Exercise 9.1
People of Influence

Focus Competencies or Practice Behaviors:

- EP 2.1.1b Practice personal reflection and self-correction to assure continual professional development
- EP 2.1.10 Engage, assess, intervene, and evaluate with individuals, families, groups, organizations, and communities

Instructions:

A. Consider all the people of influence in your community that you know or that members of your family know

B. Identify in which areas of the community they are most likely to have influence

People of Influence	Areas of Influence

Competencies/Practice Behaviors Exercise 9.2
Reality Check—A Force Field Analysis

Focus Competencies or Practice Behaviors:

- EP 2.1.7a Utilize conceptual frameworks to guide the processes of assessment, intervention, and evaluation
- EP 2.1.10e Assess client strengths and limitations

Instructions:

A. Review the salient components of a force field analysis

B. Read the scenario below, and answer each of the questions listed

> Your social work program is considering raising the grade point average needed at the time of graduation from a 2.5 to a 3.5 because some faculty members believe that grade inflation has made the 2.5 meaningless. The social work program is your community. You spend considerable time in social work classes, many of your friends are in social work, and the social work program has become the context of your sense of who you are. You have a field placement set up for next fall, and you know that your own GPA of 3.1 will probably keep you from graduating if this new change is made. (**The next exercise in this chapter will also focus on this example**.)

As a social work student in this community, do a force field analysis. Review those variables that may help or impede your attempts to stop the implementation of this proposal. Answer the following questions:

1.   Who is likely to oppose this proposal?

2.   Who is likely to benefit from it?

3.   Who is unlikely to see the proposed change as a problem?

4.   Assess the power and influence of those who support the proposal.

5.   Assess the power and influence of those who oppose the proposal.

6.   Who is the potential target in this situation?

7.   Do you think the target shares your aspirations, values, and goals? Why?

8.   How susceptible is the target to outside pressure?

Competencies/Practice Behaviors Exercise 9.3
Asset Identification

Focus Competencies or Practice Behaviors:
- EP 2.1.10e   Assess client strengths and limitations

Instructions:
A.   Refer to the situation described in the previous exercise involving a proposal to increase the minimum grade point average needed to graduate
B.   Take a position in opposition to the proposal and identify the types of assets available to you in your effort to kill this policy change
C.   Consider the following four categories of assets
   a.   Finances
   b.   People
   c.   Time
   d.   Other
D.   Follow the complete PREPARE and IMAGINE process in responding to the proposed grade point policy

Focus Competencies or Practice Behaviors:
- EP 2.1.6   Engage in research-informed practice and practice-informed research

Instructions:

A.   An important aspect of Step 1 of the PREPARE process is to carefully research the problem to be sure you have all the needed data

B.   Role play the following scenario and answer the questions at the end of this exercise

> You live in the tiny community of Kingdom Come, an idyllic-looking rural area in Michigan. The town is in an uproar after 16-year-old Estrallia Compton was killed by a fellow student, Helena Troy. Estrallia was a member of a gang of "mean girls" at school. They were a very powerful group and one student said they were, "like, rockin' with the Facebook combat!" Apparently Helena had been an online "target" of Estrallia, to the point that Helena felt the only way out was to "plug the b - - - -."
>
> A town seminar has been called to focus on these gangs and gang violence. Your group needs to research this problem to ensure that all the facts are presented at this seminar and to make sure this meeting doesn't turn into a riot.
>
> Some of the questions you need to ask are: How serious is the problem? How many people are affected? You will need to describe the problem as carefully as possible. Is there a series of problems that must be prioritized? Is this a long-standing problem that has been ignored, or one for which previous solutions have failed? What factors cause or contribute to the problem? Do cultural experiences and values dramatically affect how people view the same set of events? Are there school policies regarding bullying?

C.   After you complete the role play, cite the areas in the community that you researched. Who did you consult? Where did you find the data you needed? If data was not available, what steps did you take to find the information you needed? Who are the people affected by the problem, change agents, action systems, and target systems.

Chapter 9 Competencies/Practice Behaviors Exercises Assessment:

Name: _____ **Date:** _____
Supervisor's Name: _____

Focus Competencies/Practice Behaviors:

- EP 2.1.1b   Practice personal reflection and self-correction to assure continual professional development
- EP 2.1.6   Engage in research-informed practice and practice-informed research
- EP 2.1.7a   Utilize conceptual frameworks to guide the processes of assessment, intervention, and evaluation
- EP 2.1.10   Engage, assess, intervene, and evaluate with individuals, families, groups, organizations, and communities
- EP 2.1.10e   Assess client strengths and limitations

Instructions:

A.   Evaluate your work or your partner's work in the Focus Competencies/Practice Behaviors by completing the Competencies/Practice Behaviors Assessment form below

B.   What other Competencies/Practice Behaviors did you use to complete these Exercises? Be sure to record them in your assessments

1.	I have attained this competency/practice behavior (in the range of 81 to 100%)
2.	I have largely attained this competency/practice behavior (in the range of 61 to 80%)
3.	I have partially attained this competency/practice behavior (in the range of 41 to 60%)
4.	I have made a little progress in attaining this competency/practice behavior (in the range of 21 to 40%)
5.	I have made almost no progress in attaining this competency/practice behavior (in the range of 0 to 20%)

Student and Evaluator Assessment Scale and Comments	0	1	2	3	4	5	Agree/Disagree/Comments
EP 2.1.1 Identify as a Professional Social Worker and Conduct Oneself Accordingly							
a. Advocate for client access to the services of social work							
b. Practice personal reflection and self-correction to assure continual professional development							
c. Attend to professional roles and boundaries							
d. Demonstrate professional demeanor in behavior, appearance, and communication							
e. Engage in career-long learning							
f. Use supervision and consultation							
EP 2.1.2 Apply Social Work Ethical Principles to Guide Professional Practice							
a. Recognize and manage personal values in a way that allows professional values to guide practice							
b. Make ethical decisions by applying NASW Code of Ethics and, as applicable, of the IFSW/IASSW Ethics in Social Work, Statement of Principles							
c. Tolerate ambiguity in resolving ethical conflicts							
d. Apply strategies of ethical reasoning to arrive at principled decisions							

EP 2.1.3 Apply Critical Thinking to Inform and Communicate Professional Judgments							
a.	Distinguish, appraise, and integrate multiple sources of knowledge, including research-based knowledge and practice wisdom						
b.	Analyze models of assessment, prevention, intervention, and evaluation						
c.	Demonstrate effective oral and written communication in working with individuals, families, groups, organizations, communities, and colleagues						
EP 2.1.4 Engage Diversity and Difference in Practice							
a.	Recognize the extent to which a culture's structures and values may oppress, marginalize, alienate, or create or enhance privilege and power						
b.	Gain sufficient self-awareness to eliminate the influence of personal biases and values in working with diverse groups						
c.	Recognize and communicate their understanding of the importance of difference in shaping life experiences						
d.	View themselves as learners and engage those with whom they work as informants						
EP 2.1.5 Advance Human Rights and Social and Economic Justice							
a.	Understand forms and mechanisms of oppression and discrimination						
b.	Advocate for human rights and social and economic justice						
c.	Engage in practices that advance social and economic justice						
EP 2.1.6 Engage in Research-Informed Practice and Practice-Informed Research							
a.	Use practice experience to inform scientific inquiry						
b.	Use research evidence to inform practice						
EP 2.1.7 Apply Knowledge of Human Behavior and the Social Environment							
a.	Utilize conceptual frameworks to guide the processes of assessment, intervention, and evaluation						
b.	Critique and apply knowledge to understand person and environment						
EP 2.1.8 Engage in Policy Practice to Advance Social and Economic Well-Being and to Deliver Effective Social Work Services							
a.	Analyze, formulate, and advocate for policies that advance social well-being						
b.	Collaborate with colleagues and clients for effective policy action						
EP 2.1.9 Respond to Contexts that Shape Practice							
a.	Continuously discover, appraise, and attend to changing locales, populations, scientific and technological developments, and emerging societal trends to provide relevant services						
b.	Provide leadership in promoting sustainable changes in service delivery and practice to improve the quality of social services						

137

EP 2.1.10 Engage, Assess, Intervene, and Evaluate with Individuals, Families, Groups, Organizations and Communities						
a.	Substantively and affectively prepare for action with individuals, families, groups, organizations, and communities						
b.	Use empathy and other interpersonal skills						
c.	Develop a mutually agreed-on focus of work and desired outcomes						
d.	Collect, organize, and interpret client data						
e.	Assess client strengths and limitations						
f.	Develop mutually agreed-on intervention goals and objectives						
g.	Select appropriate intervention strategies						
h.	Initiate actions to achieve organizational goals						
i.	Implement prevention interventions that enhance client capacities						
j.	Help clients resolve problems						
k.	Negotiate, mediate, and advocate for clients						
l.	Facilitate transitions and endings						
m.	Critically analyze, monitor, and evaluate interventions						

Competencies/Practice Behaviors Exercise 10.1
Key Concepts

Focus Competencies or Practice Behaviors:
- EP 2.1.7a   Utilize conceptual frameworks to guide the processes of assessment, intervention, and evaluation
- EP 2.1.7b   Critique and apply knowledge to understand person and environment

Instructions:

A.   In the text, study the key concepts involved in evaluating macro practice, including the difference between descriptive and inferential statistics and the characteristics of random sampling

B.   Read the questions contained in the box below and answer each question

Questions to Consider:

A recent report said that the average age of residents in a small nursing home was 72 and most residents were women. Are the statistics used here likely to be descriptive or inferential? Why?

The community of Plantwart has an average per capita income of $15,000 while the neighboring community of Nosegay has a per capita income of $16,000. A friend says there is a real difference of $1000 between the two communities but the difference is not statistically significant. What does she mean by this?

A polling organization is using sampling to gather opinions about voting preferences from members of your community. If every person in your community has an equal chance of being selected to participate in the study, what type of sampling is being used?

Competencies/Practice Behaviors Exercise 10.2
Program Objectives

Focus Competencies or Practice Behaviors:
- EP 2.1.10f   Develop mutually agreed-on intervention goals and objectives
- EP 2.1.10m   Critically analyze, monitor, and evaluate interventions

Instructions:
A.   Review material on designing measurable objectives
B.   Read the information in the box below and answer both of the following questions

---

Your field agency has a stated objective for its family enrichment program that reads as follows:

"We will help each client improve his or her life."

1.   What potential problems might the agency have in evaluating its effectiveness in meeting this objective?

2.   How would you improve the objective? Write out your suggestion.

Competencies/Practice Behaviors Exercise 10.3
Keeping It All Straight

Focus Competencies or Practice Behaviors:
- EP 2.1.7a   Utilize conceptual frameworks to guide the processes of assessment, intervention, and evaluation
- EP 2.1.7b   Critique and apply knowledge to understand person and environment

Instructions:
A.   Read the various evaluation and research concepts in the text
B.   Match the following concepts with the corresponding description

1. Baseline _____
2. Control Group _____
3. Experimental Group _____
4. Dependent Variable _____
5. Independent Variable _____
6. Sampling _____
7. Random Sample _____
8. Experimental Design _____
9. Quasi-Experimental Design _____
10. Mean _____

11. Median _____
12. Mode _____
13. Standard Deviation _____
14. Reliability _____
15. Validity _____
16. Descriptive Statistics _____
17. Inferential Statistics _____
18. Outcome _____
19. Statistical Significance _____
20. Chi-Square Test _____

A. A statistical procedure for comparing expected and observed frequencies.
B. The most frequently observed score in a group of scores.
C. A group used for comparison purposes.
D. Using a subset of all clients seen by an agency rather than surveying the entire group.
E. The group receiving an intervention.
F. A design using control and experimental groups but not random assignment.
G. The original amount or occurrence of a behavior or event.
H. The behavior intervention is intended to change.
I. The ability of an instrument to measure what it is supposed to measure.
J. The arithmetic average of a group of numbers.
K. A measure of the variability of a group of scores around a mean.
L. A quality of life change resulting from social work intervention.
M. The risk involved generalizing from a sample to the population as a whole.
N. Statistics used to draw a conclusion about a population based on a sample of that population.
O. The middle figure in a distribution of figures listed from highest to lowest or vice versa.
P. The likelihood that a measurement will yield the same results at subsequent times.
Q. The average age of a group of delinquent youth, for example.
R. A social work intervention is an example of this type of variable.
S. A subset chosen so that all members of the population have an equal chance of being selected.
T. An elaborate method for evaluating an intervention; includes control groups, experimental groups, and random assignment of clients to one group or the other.

Focus Competencies or Practice Behaviors:
- EP 2.1.10m   Critically analyze, monitor, and evaluate interventions

Instructions:
A.   After studying the evaluation tools in this chapter in the text, read the four vignettes
B.   Identify those situations that can be evaluated
C.   Identify any vignettes where evaluation is not possible
D.   Provide reasons for your decisions

You will often have the opportunity to evaluate, but you may decide that some efforts simply are not necessary. Look at the following four vignettes, then decide which you would evaluate and explain why or why not.

Vignette 1: Nathan House Renovation
   Nathan House is a shelter for runaways that is operated by your agency. A local service organization has offered to renovate Nathan House over a six-month period. Renovations will include paint, new carpeting and furniture, and new lighting. Would you evaluate this intervention? Explain your answer.

Vignette 2: Nathan House Legal Education Program
   Runaways at Nathan House are expected to participate in a legal education program designed to make them aware of their rights and obligations under the law. The program is founded on the idea that residents will be less likely to get into further trouble if they understand the law. Should you attempt to evaluate this program? Why or why not?

Vignette 3: Drug Abuse Community Education Program
Nathan House is one of several agencies offering all residents an opportunity to learn about drugs and thus to help reduce the levels of drug abuse in the community. The program is based on a national model in use in other states and will begin in about six weeks. Would you recommend evaluating this program? Give your reasons.

Vignette 4: Council of Agency Executives Group
Your agency director is part of a new group composed of executives of all agencies serving adolescents in the community. The group meets once a month to share information and discuss community-wide problems. The director asks you if you think this group should be evaluated. Should this group's efforts be evaluated? Discuss your reasons.

Competencies/Practice Behaviors Exercise 10.5
Designing an Evaluation Program

Focus Competencies or Practice Behaviors:
- EP 2.1.10m   Critically analyze, monitor, and evaluate interventions

Instructions:
A.   Review the section in the text on program evaluation approaches
B.   Read each of the scenarios below and discuss how you would evaluate the program

1:      Evaluating Hospital Discharge Planning: You are the Director of Social Services at Our Lady of Perpetual Misery Hospital. Your unit is primarily involved in doing discharge planning, with three BSW social workers assigned to this function. Discharge planning involves working with the hospital medical staff to facilitate patients' transition following discharge. Typically, your unit helps clients return to their own homes, go to nursing homes for temporary care or on a permanent basis, or go to live with relatives. Your unit uses a variety of community services including transportation, medical equipment for use in the home, visiting nurses, home health care, and similar services. The hospital administrator has asked all directors to begin to consider how they might evaluate the effectiveness of their units. You want to develop an evaluation program that can be done with existing staff, does not intrude on your work with patients, and is relatively simple to implement. Explain the methods you will use to evaluate your unit's effectiveness.

2:      Evaluating a Hospice Care Program: Your hospice program has been funded by the county for its first year of operation. As a condition of continued funding, you must develop an evaluation component that will allow the funding source to determine whether to continue your program next year. Patients come to you from area hospitals, nursing homes, and from their own homes. All are suffering from terminal illnesses ranging from AIDS to cancer to other life-ending diseases. Your hospice provides services to in-patients and to people in their own homes. Your evaluation plan should provide the county with data to justify your continued funding.

3:      Evaluating an Assertiveness Training Group: Your agency operates assertiveness training groups for women who are survivors of domestic violence. Each group lasts four weeks and consists of 6-8 women per group. You lead this group and are curious about whether members really become more assertive after leaving the group. Design an evaluation system that would help you answer this question.

Focus Competencies or Practice Behaviors:
- EP 2.1.10m   Critically analyze, monitor, and evaluate interventions

Instructions:
A.   Review the section in the text on program evaluation approaches
B.   Read the scenario below and role play how to evaluate the program

> Your group has helped the Green Oak neighborhood develop a neighborhood watch program to combat the many burglaries and auto thefts suffered by area residents. The police department was very cooperative in helping you establish this program, but your agency director isn't convinced that these kinds of programs are worthwhile. He questions why your unit spends their time on such activities. Your unit is meeting to discuss designing an evaluation program to show that this type of program is effective in reducing crime.

C.   After the role play, answer the following questions:

1.   Which evaluation design did you decide to use?

2.   Why did you decide NOT to use the other designs?

3.   What information will you provide in this evaluation?

4.   How will you collect the data?

5.   What types of graphics will you use and how will this be presented to your agency director?

Chapter 10 Competencies/Practice Behaviors Exercises Assessment:

Name: _____ **Date:** _____

Supervisor's Name: _____

Focus Competencies/Practice Behaviors:
- EP 2.1.7a   Utilize conceptual frameworks to guide the processes of assessment, intervention, and evaluation
- EP 2.1.7b   Critique and apply knowledge to understand person and environment
- EP 2.1.10f   Develop mutually agreed-on intervention goals and objectives
- EP 2.1.10m   Critically analyze, monitor, and evaluate interventions

Instructions:

A.   Evaluate your work or your partner's work in the Focus Competencies/Practice Behaviors by completing the Competencies/Practice Behaviors Assessment form below

B.   What other Competencies/Practice Behaviors did you use to complete these Exercises? Be sure to record them in your assessments

1.	I have attained this competency/practice behavior (in the range of 81 to 100%)
2.	I have largely attained this competency/practice behavior (in the range of 61 to 80%)
3.	I have partially attained this competency/practice behavior (in the range of 41 to 60%)
4.	I have made a little progress in attaining this competency/practice behavior (in the range of 21 to 40%)
5.	I have made almost no progress in attaining this competency/practice behavior (in the range of 0 to 20%)

Student and Evaluator Assessment Scale and Comments	0	1	2	3	4	5	Agree/Disagree/Comments
EP 2.1.1 Identify as a Professional Social Worker and Conduct Oneself Accordingly							
a. Advocate for client access to the services of social work							
b. Practice personal reflection and self-correction to assure continual professional development							
c. Attend to professional roles and boundaries							
d. Demonstrate professional demeanor in behavior, appearance, and communication							
e. Engage in career-long learning							
f. Use supervision and consultation							
EP 2.1.2 Apply Social Work Ethical Principles to Guide Professional Practice							
a. Recognize and manage personal values in a way that allows professional values to guide practice							
b. Make ethical decisions by applying NASW Code of Ethics and, as applicable, of the IFSW/IASSW Ethics in Social Work, Statement of Principles							
c. Tolerate ambiguity in resolving ethical conflicts							
d. Apply strategies of ethical reasoning to arrive at principled decisions							

EP 2.1.3 Apply Critical Thinking to Inform and Communicate Professional Judgments							
a. Distinguish, appraise, and integrate multiple sources of knowledge, including research-based knowledge and practice wisdom							
b. Analyze models of assessment, prevention, intervention, and evaluation							
c. Demonstrate effective oral and written communication in working with individuals, families, groups, organizations, communities, and colleagues							
EP 2.1.4 Engage Diversity and Difference in Practice							
a. Recognize the extent to which a culture's structures and values may oppress, marginalize, alienate, or create or enhance privilege and power							
b. Gain sufficient self-awareness to eliminate the influence of personal biases and values in working with diverse groups							
c. Recognize and communicate their understanding of the importance of difference in shaping life experiences							
d. View themselves as learners and engage those with whom they work as informants							
EP 2.1.5 Advance Human Rights and Social and Economic Justice							
a. Understand forms and mechanisms of oppression and discrimination							
b. Advocate for human rights and social and economic justice							
c. Engage in practices that advance social and economic justice							
EP 2.1.6 Engage in Research-Informed Practice and Practice-Informed Research							
a. Use practice experience to inform scientific inquiry							
b. Use research evidence to inform practice							
EP 2.1.7 Apply Knowledge of Human Behavior and the Social Environment							
a. Utilize conceptual frameworks to guide the processes of assessment, intervention, and evaluation							
b. Critique and apply knowledge to understand person and environment							
EP 2.1.8 Engage in Policy Practice to Advance Social and Economic Well-Being and to Deliver Effective Social Work Services							
a. Analyze, formulate, and advocate for policies that advance social well-being							
b. Collaborate with colleagues and clients for effective policy action							
EP 2.1.9 Respond to Contexts that Shape Practice							
a. Continuously discover, appraise, and attend to changing locales, populations, scientific and technological developments, and emerging societal trends to provide relevant services							
b. Provide leadership in promoting sustainable changes in service delivery and practice to							

improve the quality of social services							
EP 2.1.10 Engage, Assess, Intervene, and Evaluate with Individuals, Families, Groups, Organizations and Communities							
a. Substantively and affectively prepare for action with individuals, families, groups, organizations, and communities							
b. Use empathy and other interpersonal skills							
c. Develop a mutually agreed-on focus of work and desired outcomes							
d. Collect, organize, and interpret client data							
e. Assess client strengths and limitations							
f. Develop mutually agreed-on intervention goals and objectives							
g. Select appropriate intervention strategies							
h. Initiate actions to achieve organizational goals							
i. Implement prevention interventions that enhance client capacities							
j. Help clients resolve problems							
k. Negotiate, mediate, and advocate for clients							
l. Facilitate transitions and endings							
m. Critically analyze, monitor, and evaluate interventions							

Competencies/Practice Behaviors Exercise 11.1
Populations-At-Risk

Focus Competencies or Practice Behaviors:
- EP 2.1.5a   Understand forms and mechanisms of oppression and discrimination
- EP 2.1.7a   Utilize conceptual frameworks to guide the processes of assessment, intervention, and evaluation

Instructions:
A.   Identify at least five populations-at-risk served by social workers
B.   What places these populations at risk?

Competencies/Practice Behaviors Exercise 11.2
Recalling Key Concepts

Focus Competencies or Practice Behaviors:
- EP 2.1.7a   Utilize conceptual frameworks to guide the processes of assessment, intervention, and evaluation
- EP 2.1.7b   Critique and apply knowledge to understand person and environment

Instructions:
A.   Review each of the case situations shown below
B.   Recalling key concepts from the text, respond to the questions following the cases

> Miguel Gonzales is a social worker with A Family Affair, a counseling service for couples and families. During one of his sessions with the Chou Vang family, recent immigrants from Southeast Asia, he learns that the Vang children have been prevented from using the community swimming pool. According to Mrs. Vang, one of the lifeguards has called her children names and said they should go back to their own country. Miguel offers to help the family deal with this situation and agrees to talk to the city's recreation director who oversees the pool. Using the information given, answer each of the following queries.

149

1.   Is Miguel engaged in cause advocacy or case advocacy as he seeks to help the Vang family? Explain your answer.

Miguel discovers that the director of recreation believes that the Vang children and other Hmong refugees should not be using the pool because they are not yet U.S. citizens. Miguel decides to challenge the director's decision by enlisting the help of the local Urban League. Together, they picket the swimming pool and invite the media to cover the event.

2.   Does Miguel's strategy fall under the classification of social action? Why or why not?

3.   What would be needed to empower the Vang family to solve this problem by themselves?

4.   Do you consider the Vang family a population-at-risk? Explain your answer.

Competencies/Practice Behaviors Exercise 11.3
Assessing Your Experience as an Advocate

Focus Competencies or Practice Behaviors:
- EP 2.1.1b   Practice personal reflection and self-correction to assure continual professional development

Instructions:
A.   Think about advocacy situations you have encountered in your life
B.   Review the following paragraph and respond to the questions listed

In the past you've probably come across situations when it was necessary to advocate for yourself or others.

1.   Describe such situation you encountered and list the actions you took.

2.   If you took no action, what considerations led you to decide not to act?

3.   What was the eventual outcome?

4.   Looking back, what do you think you should have done to increase your effectiveness?

Competencies/Practice Behaviors Exercise 11.4
Using Advocacy Tactics

Focus Competencies or Practice Behaviors:
- EP 2.1.5b   Advocate for human rights and social economic justice

Instructions:
A.   Based on the information given in each of the scenarios below, indicate which advocacy tactics might be most appropriate
B.   Explain your choices for each

Scenario 1: The state legislature is taking up the issue of property tax reform and is considering shifting financial responsibility for certain public assistance programs from the local community to the state. This would result in lower property taxes for everyone in the community but higher income taxes. You believe this would make the method of paying for welfare fairer and more progressive.

Select the advocacy tactic that seems most appropriate for this situation and explain your choice.

Scenario 2: Neighbors in the Elm Terrace section of your community are upset by a proposal to widen their street to allow larger trucks into the area. Many residents are elderly, low-income, and politically inexperienced.

Select the advocacy tactic you would use to oppose this proposal. Explain why you chose this tactic.

Scenario 4: Rosa Daniels has been suspended from school because she came to class wearing her hair in the braided fashion popular in Jamaica. Other teenagers are free to wear their hair in the latest fashion. However, the school's principal believes Rosa's hairdo is a sign of gang affiliation.

If you were to advise the Daniels family, which advocacy tactic would you suggest and why?

Competencies/Practice Behaviors Exercise 11.5
Role Play Using Advocacy Tactics

Focus Competencies or Practice Behaviors:
- EP 2.1.5a   Understand forms and mechanisms of oppression and discrimination
- EP 2.1.5b   Advocate for human rights and social economic justice

Instructions:

A.   Based on the information given in the scenario below, role play which advocacy tactics might be most appropriate

B.   You should each pick a tactic and persuade the group that your idea is the best

> **Scenario 3:** Your agency director has been asked to hire at least one new Spanish-speaking worker to work with the growing Hispanic population served by your organization. He isn't convinced that there is sufficient justification for such a hire. He has kicked the issue down to your unit for input because your have been asking for this Spanish-speaking worker for a long time.

Chapter 11 Competencies/Practice Behaviors Exercises Assessment:

Name: _____ **Date:** _____

Supervisor's Name: _____

Focus Competencies/Practice Behaviors:

- EP 2.1.1b   Practice personal reflection and self-correction to assure continual professional development
- EP 2.1.5a   Understand forms and mechanisms of oppression and discrimination
- EP 2.1.5b   Advocate for human rights and social and economic justice
- EP 2.1.7a   Utilize conceptual frameworks to guide the processes of assessment, intervention, and evaluation
- EP 2.1.7b   Critique and apply knowledge to understand person and environment

Instructions:

A.   Evaluate your work or your partner's work in the Focus Competencies/Practice Behaviors by completing the Competencies/Practice Behaviors Assessment form below

B.   What other Competencies/Practice Behaviors did you use to complete these Exercises? Be sure to record them in your assessments

1.	I have attained this competency/practice behavior (in the range of 81 to 100%)
2.	I have largely attained this competency/practice behavior (in the range of 61 to 80%)
3.	I have partially attained this competency/practice behavior (in the range of 41 to 60%)
4.	I have made a little progress in attaining this competency/practice behavior (in the range of 21 to 40%)
5.	I have made almost no progress in attaining this competency/practice behavior (in the range of 0 to 20%)

Student and Evaluator Assessment Scale and Comments	0	1	2	3	4	5	Agree/Disagree/Comments
EP 2.1.1 Identify as a Professional Social Worker and Conduct Oneself Accordingly							
a. Advocate for client access to the services of social work							
b. Practice personal reflection and self-correction to assure continual professional development							
c. Attend to professional roles and boundaries							
d. Demonstrate professional demeanor in behavior, appearance, and communication							
e. Engage in career-long learning							
f. Use supervision and consultation							
EP 2.1.2 Apply Social Work Ethical Principles to Guide Professional Practice							
a. Recognize and manage personal values in a way that allows professional values to guide practice							
b. Make ethical decisions by applying NASW Code of Ethics and, as applicable, of the IFSW/IASSW Ethics in Social Work, Statement of Principles							
c. Tolerate ambiguity in resolving ethical conflicts							
d. Apply strategies of ethical reasoning to arrive at principled decisions							

154

EP 2.1.3 Apply Critical Thinking to Inform and Communicate Professional Judgments							
a. Distinguish, appraise, and integrate multiple sources of knowledge, including research-based knowledge and practice wisdom							
b. Analyze models of assessment, prevention, intervention, and evaluation							
c. Demonstrate effective oral and written communication in working with individuals, families, groups, organizations, communities, and colleagues							
EP 2.1.4 Engage Diversity and Difference in Practice							
a. Recognize the extent to which a culture's structures and values may oppress, marginalize, alienate, or create or enhance privilege and power							
b. Gain sufficient self-awareness to eliminate the influence of personal biases and values in working with diverse groups							
c. Recognize and communicate their understanding of the importance of difference in shaping life experiences							
d. View themselves as learners and engage those with whom they work as informants							
EP 2.1.5 Advance Human Rights and Social and Economic Justice							
a. Understand forms and mechanisms of oppression and discrimination							
b. Advocate for human rights and social and economic justice							
c. Engage in practices that advance social and economic justice							
EP 2.1.6 Engage in Research-Informed Practice and Practice-Informed Research							
a. Use practice experience to inform scientific inquiry							
b. Use research evidence to inform practice							
EP 2.1.7 Apply Knowledge of Human Behavior and the Social Environment							
a. Utilize conceptual frameworks to guide the processes of assessment, intervention, and evaluation							
b. Critique and apply knowledge to understand person and environment							
EP 2.1.8 Engage in Policy Practice to Advance Social and Economic Well-Being and to Deliver Effective Social Work Services							
a. Analyze, formulate, and advocate for policies that advance social well-being							
b. Collaborate with colleagues and clients for effective policy action							
EP 2.1.9 Respond to Contexts that Shape Practice							
a. Continuously discover, appraise, and attend to changing locales, populations, scientific and technological developments, and emerging societal trends to provide relevant services							
b. Provide leadership in promoting sustainable changes in service delivery and practice to improve the quality of social services							

155

EP 2.1.10 Engage, Assess, Intervene, and Evaluate with Individuals, Families, Groups, Organizations and Communities						
a.	Substantively and affectively prepare for action with individuals, families, groups, organizations, and communities						
b.	Use empathy and other interpersonal skills						
c.	Develop a mutually agreed-on focus of work and desired outcomes						
d.	Collect, organize, and interpret client data						
e.	Assess client strengths and limitations						
f.	Develop mutually agreed-on intervention goals and objectives						
g.	Select appropriate intervention strategies						
h.	Initiate actions to achieve organizational goals						
i.	Implement prevention interventions that enhance client capacities						
j.	Help clients resolve problems						
k.	Negotiate, mediate, and advocate for clients						
l.	Facilitate transitions and endings						
m.	Critically analyze, monitor, and evaluate interventions						

Competencies/Practice Behaviors Exercise 12.1
NASW Code of Ethics

Focus Competencies or Practice Behaviors:
- EP 2.1.2b   Make ethical decisions by applying standards of the National Association of Social Workers Code of Ethics and, as applicable, of the International Federation of Social Workers/International Association of Schools of Social Work Ethics in Social Work, Statement of Principles

Instructions:
A.   The six core values in the NASW Code of Ethics include: (1) service, (2) social justice, (3) dignity and worth of the person, (4) the importance of human relationships, (5) integrity, and (6) competence. Define each of these concepts in your own words
B.   How does each relate to the Dolgoff et al. (2005) hierarchy of ethical principles?

Focus Competencies or Practice Behaviors:
- ☛ EP 2.1.2a   Recognize and manage personal values in a way that allows professional values to guide practice
- ● EP 2.1.2b   Make ethical decisions by applying standards of the National Association of Social Workers Code of Ethics and, as applicable, of the International Federation of Social Workers/International Association of Schools of Social Work Ethics in Social Work, Statement of Principles
- ● EP 2.1.2c   Tolerate ambiguity in resolving ethical conflicts
- ● EP 2.1.2d   Apply strategies of ethical reasoning to arrive at principled decisions

Instructions:
A.   Review the Ethical Principles Screen (Ethics for U) in the text and the various ethical dilemmas in macro contexts that social workers might encounter
B.   Apply Ethics for U to each problematic vignette and propose a viable solution

> *CASE SCENARIO A (Distributing Limited Resources):* The family services agency where you work counseling survivors of domestic violence has suffered significant budget cuts. The agency administration has indicated that it will eliminate some services in order to stay afloat. Potentially targeted programs include day-care for working parents, sex education and contraception counseling for teens, or the thriving but expensive foreign adoptions program. The agency's other alternatives might include elimination of your own domestic violence program, decreasing staff for all programs including your own, or significantly cutting workers' salaries (including your own) across the board.
>
> The community has depended on your agency's provision of its various services for many years. Thus, adequate alternate services do not exist in your community.

1.   Which principles in *ETHICS for U* might apply to this situation?

2.   How can you use the Ethical Principles Screen in deciding how best to cut expenses?

3.   As a social worker, what would *you* do in this situation?

CASE SCENARIO B (Colleagues' Sexual Involvement with Clients): You see a professional colleague engaging in what you consider unethical behavior. Twice you have seen him out in the community on dates with women you know to be his clients. It would be very uncomfortable for you to confront him about this behavior. Informing your supervisor seems like tattling.

---

1.   Which ethical principles in *ETHICS for U* might apply to this situation?

2.   How can you use the principles' ranking in deciding what to do in this situation?

3.   As a social worker, what would *you* do in this situation?

CASE SCENARIO C (Whistle-blowing): (*Whistle-blowing* is the act of informing on another or making public an individual's, group's or organization's corrupt, wrong, illegal, inefficient, or hazardous behavior.) You are a public assistance worker facing an ethical dilemma concerning whether or not to blow the whistle on a newly promoted supervisor (Reamer, 1990). You have worked at the agency for almost two years, and you are increasingly frustrated by the attitudes and work habits of a number of your immediate colleagues. They seem to spend as little time as possible with clients, even denying them necessary and appropriate assistance if the worker doesn't have time to complete all the necessary paperwork. In other cases, workers bend the rules to give clients benefits to which they are not entitled. For instance, many clients work as domestic help and are paid in cash, and workers do not always report all the clients' income. Workers simply make decisions according to their own discretion. Additionally, you note that workers consistently pad their travel expense accounts.

You are appalled by this behavior, and although you don't like the thought of "making waves," you finally confide your concerns to your friend and colleague Zenda. Zenda "pooh-poohs" your concerns condescendingly, remarking that such violations bend rules that aren't very good to begin with. She explains that such worker discretion is really an informal agency policy and adds that padding travel expense accounts is universally accepted as a means of increasing workers' relatively meager salaries. Zenda tries to soothe you and arrest your concerns, but it doesn't work. You decide that from now on you had best keep your concerns to yourself until you can figure out what to do about them.

Abruptly you find out that Zenda has been promoted and is your new unit supervisor. You are stunned. How can Zenda maintain order and help supervisees follow agency and other regulations when Zenda herself typically violates them?

What can you do? Ignore the whole situation? Confront your colleagues about their behavior? Confront Zenda again, even though it did no good the first time? Report your concerns to someone higher up in the administration? If you do and Zenda considers you a traitor, how miserable can Zenda make your life as an employee? Should you report the problem to NASW or the State Licensing Board? Should you blow the whistle to the press? How long do you think you'll keep your job if you take the problem outside established agency channels? Should you quit?

1. Discuss which principles in *ETHICS for U* might apply to this situation?

2. How can you use the principles' ranking to come to a decision?

3.   As a social worker, what would *you* do in this situation?

CASE SCENARIO D (Racist Individual and Organizational Behavior): The private social service agency you work for does not have a formal affirmative action policy for hiring personnel. You have heard the agency director make several lewd racial remarks and jokes. You cannot believe he has gotten away with it. You have only worked for the agency for three months of your six-month probationary period, so you could be dismissed in the blink of an eye. The agency has no minorities of color on staff though it has clients who are minorities of color.[1] You believe that recruiting staff who are minorities of color is essential to the agency's ability to perform its functions. You also think the staff and the agency director need feedback in order to change their prejudicial and discriminatory behavior.

What is your role? Should you look away and pretend you don't know anything is wrong? Should you charge into the Director's office like a bull in a china shop and complain? Can you talk to other staff to see what they think? Should you contact the agency's board of directors? Should you contact the press or some external regulatory agency and blow the whistle? Should you quit your job?

---

1.   Which principles in *ETHICS for U* might apply to this situation?

2.   How can you use the principles' ranking to come to a decision?

---

[1]*Minority* is "one term for a group, or a member of a group, of people of a distinct racial, religious, ethnic, or political identity that is smaller or less powerful than the community's controlling group" (Barker, 2003, p. 274). The term *minorities of color* concerns "people who have minority status because their skin color differs from that of the community's predominant group. In the United States, the term usually refers to African Americans, Asian Americans, American Indians, and certain other minority groups" (Barker, 2003, p. 274).

3.   As a social worker, what would *you* do in this situation?

CASE SCENARIO E (Initiating Community Action "Against the Flow"): The community in which you live and work provides no services for homeless people, despite the fact that their numbers are escalating. Every day on your way to and from work you pass at least a half dozen people roaming the urban streets. Many times you see children with them, dirty, probably hungry, and obviously not in school. Most people at your agency don't really want to talk about it. You get the feeling that colleagues, supervisors, and administrators think they have enough to do already. Work demands continue to increase while funding resources shrink.

---

1.   Which ethical principles in *ETHICS for U* might apply to this situation?

2.   How can you use the principles' ranking to come to a decision?

3.   As a social worker, what would *you* do in this situation?

CASE SCENARIO F (Lack of Community Support): You are a worker at a rural county social services agency. You, other colleagues, and agency administration have identified a significant lesbian and gay population in the area. You and the other professionals would like to implement a new program providing support groups for lesbian and gay people dealing with several issues, including single parenthood, legal difficulties such as housing discrimination, and other issues. Several relatively powerful members of the County Board get wind of your idea and react with almost violent frenzy. They band together with a number of citizens who adamantly refuse to allow expenditure of public resources on lesbian and gay people.

1. Which principles in *ETHICS for U* might apply to this situation?

2. How can you use the principles' ranking in coming to a decision?

3. As a social worker, what would you do in this situation?

Focus Competencies or Practice Behaviors:
- EP 2.1.2d   Apply strategies of ethical reasoning to arrive at principled decisions

Instructions:
A.   Review the Dolgoff et al. (2005) Ethical Principles Screen
B.   You and your classmates will assume the role of Marvin, Samantha, and Grisella
C.   Role play the case situation below and write a summary of your conclusion to this ethical dilemma using the Ethical Principles Screen by Dolgoff et al.

Using Ethical Screens

Samantha is a social worker in Dalanta County. She has an excessively large case load. On Friday afternoon she has an appointment with Marvin H. Marv has been coming to Samantha for three weeks. He has been "down in the dumps" for a few months and three weeks ago his girlfriend, Carmin told him to "get over it or get out!"

Marv comes in and Samantha (his social worker) can tell he is very agitated. He tells her he intends to hurt Carmin, who he says "dumped him" for another guy.

According to the Dolgoff et al. (2005) Ethical Principles Screen, a client has a right to autonomy and self-determination, confidentiality and privacy. Yet Samantha is concerned about possible harm to Marvin's ex-girlfriend, Carmin. What principles from the ethical screen would apply here?

Grisella (Samantha's supervisor) informs Samantha about the agency's policy that attempts to ensure absolute confidentiality to clients and discourages workers from talking about cases with other agencies without a written release of information from the client. What is Samantha to do?

---

1.   What are the dilemmas experienced in this role play?

2.   How were they expressed?

3.   How were these dilemmas resolved?

4.   What are your thoughts about this dilemma?

Chapter 12 Competencies or Practice Behaviors Exercises Assessment:

Name: _____ **Date:** _____

Supervisor's Name: _____

Focus Competencies/Practice Behaviors:

- EP 2.1.2a   Recognize and manage personal values in a way that allows professional values to guide practice
- EP 2.1.2b   Make ethical decisions by applying standards of the National Association of Social Workers Code of Ethics and, as applicable, of the International Federation of Social Workers/International Association of Schools of Social Work Ethics in Social Work, Statement of Principles
- EP 2.1.2c   Tolerate ambiguity in resolving ethical conflicts
- EP 2.1.2d   Apply strategies of ethical reasoning to arrive at principled decisions

Instructions:

A.   Evaluate your work or your partner's work in the Focus Competencies/Practice Behaviors by completing the Competencies/Practice Behaviors Assessment form below

B.   What other Competencies/Practice Behaviors did you use to complete these Exercises? Be sure to record them in your assessments

1.	I have attained this competency/practice behavior (in the range of 81 to 100%)
2.	I have largely attained this competency/practice behavior (in the range of 61 to 80%)
3.	I have partially attained this competency/practice behavior (in the range of 41 to 60%)
4.	I have made a little progress in attaining this competency/practice behavior (in the range of 21 to 40%)
5.	I have made almost no progress in attaining this competency/practice behavior (in the range of 0 to 20%)

EPAS 2008 Core Competencies & Core Practice Behaviors	Student Self Assessment						Evaluator Feedback
Student and Evaluator Assessment Scale and Comments	0	1	2	3	4	5	Agree/Disagree/Comments
EP 2.1.1 Identify as a Professional Social Worker and Conduct Oneself Accordingly							
a. Advocate for client access to the services of social work							
b. Practice personal reflection and self-correction to assure continual professional development							
c. Attend to professional roles and boundaries							
d. Demonstrate professional demeanor in behavior, appearance, and communication							
e. Engage in career-long learning							
f. Use supervision and consultation							
EP 2.1.2 Apply Social Work Ethical Principles to Guide Professional Practice							
a. Recognize and manage personal values in a way that allows professional values to guide practice							
b. Make ethical decisions by applying NASW Code of Ethics and, as applicable, of the IFSW/IASSW Ethics in Social Work, Statement of Principles							
c. Tolerate ambiguity in resolving ethical conflicts							
d. Apply strategies of ethical reasoning to arrive at principled decisions							

EP 2.1.3 Apply Critical Thinking to Inform and Communicate Professional Judgments							
a.	Distinguish, appraise, and integrate multiple sources of knowledge, including research-based knowledge and practice wisdom						
b.	Analyze models of assessment, prevention, intervention, and evaluation						
c.	Demonstrate effective oral and written communication in working with individuals, families, groups, organizations, communities, and colleagues						
EP 2.1.4 Engage Diversity and Difference in Practice							
a.	Recognize the extent to which a culture's structures and values may oppress, marginalize, alienate, or create or enhance privilege and power						
b.	Gain sufficient self-awareness to eliminate the influence of personal biases and values in working with diverse groups						
c.	Recognize and communicate their understanding of the importance of difference in shaping life experiences						
d.	View themselves as learners and engage those with whom they work as informants						
EP 2.1.5 Advance Human Rights and Social and Economic Justice							
a.	Understand forms and mechanisms of oppression and discrimination						
b.	Advocate for human rights and social and economic justice						
c.	Engage in practices that advance social and economic justice						
EP 2.1.6 Engage in Research-Informed Practice and Practice-Informed Research							
a.	Use practice experience to inform scientific inquiry						
b.	Use research evidence to inform practice						
EP 2.1.7 Apply Knowledge of Human Behavior and the Social Environment							
a.	Utilize conceptual frameworks to guide the processes of assessment, intervention, and evaluation						
b.	Critique and apply knowledge to understand person and environment						
EP 2.1.8 Engage in Policy Practice to Advance Social and Economic Well-Being and to Deliver Effective Social Work Services							
a.	Analyze, formulate, and advocate for policies that advance social well-being						
b.	Collaborate with colleagues and clients for effective policy action						
EP 2.1.9 Respond to Contexts that Shape Practice							
a.	Continuously discover, appraise, and attend to changing locales, populations, scientific and technological developments, and emerging societal trends to provide relevant services						
b.	Provide leadership in promoting sustainable changes in service delivery and practice to improve the quality of social services						

EP 2.1.10 Engage, Assess, Intervene, and Evaluate with Individuals, Families, Groups, Organizations and Communities						
a.	Substantively and affectively prepare for action with individuals, families, groups, organizations, and communities					
b.	Use empathy and other interpersonal skills					
c.	Develop a mutually agreed-on focus of work and desired outcomes					
d.	Collect, organize, and interpret client data					
e.	Assess client strengths and limitations					
f.	Develop mutually agreed-on intervention goals and objectives					
g.	Select appropriate intervention strategies					
h.	Initiate actions to achieve organizational goals					
i.	Implement prevention interventions that enhance client capacities					
j.	Help clients resolve problems					
k.	Negotiate, mediate, and advocate for clients					
l.	Facilitate transitions and endings					
m.	Critically analyze, monitor, and evaluate interventions					

Competencies/Practice Behaviors Exercise 13.1
Understanding Court Terminology

Focus Competencies or Practice Behaviors:

- EP 2.1.7b   Critique and apply knowledge to understand person and environment

Instructions:

A.   Read the text regarding concepts of court terminology

B.   Match the following concepts concerning goals with their respective meanings

1.	Criminal violation	_____
2.	Jurisdiction	_____
3.	Allegation	_____
4.	Disposition	_____
5.	Due process	_____
6.	Stipulation	_____
7.	Burden of proof	_____
8.	Standards of proof	_____
9.	Real evidence	_____
10.	Documentary evidence	_____
11.	Testimony	_____
12.	Hearsay evidence	_____
13.	Civil offense	_____
14.	Misdemeanor	_____
15.	Felony	_____
16.	Confidentiality	_____
17.	Privileged communication	_____
18.	Subpoena	_____

a.	An agreement by both parties on a point of information or fact that pertains to the proceedings or trial.
b.	The principle that information shared between the client and social worker is intended to be kept private.
c.	A legal writ ordering an individual to appear in court to testify regarding a client, often requiring that written documents be brought along as well.
d.	An offense penalized by fine and/or imprisonment.
e.	A violation for which the sole penalty is forfeiture of money or goods.
f.	A less serious crime considered serious enough to be punishable by imprisonment for a term of one or more years.
g.	Authority to act.
h.	The requirement that law in its regular course of administration must document that it guarantees the protection of a fair trial.
i.	Testimony about a statement made outside the courtroom.
j.	The condition that it is the responsibility of the party making the complaint to prove the allegations set out in the petition filed before the court.
k.	Information shared between the client and another party that is protected by state statute.

l.   The assertion of one side in a lawsuit setting out what that party expects to prove at the trial.

m.   Evidence consisting of tangible objects such as weapons or photographs.

n.   The second phase of the court process where the sentence is determined.

o.   The level or degree of certainty needed to prove an allegation in court.

p.   The actual interviewing of a witness by the defendant or, more typically, his or her attorney.

q.   Certified documents usually identified and authenticated by proper authorities.

r.   A crime considered serious enough to be punishable by imprisonment for a term of one or more years.

Competencies/Practice Behaviors Exercise 13.2
Courtroom Protocol and Social Work Practice

Focus Competencies or Practice Behaviors:
- EP 2.1.1d   Demonstrate professional demeanor in behavior, appearance, and communication

Instructions:

A.   Read the text regarding social work practice and courtroom protocol

B.   After reading the vignette, identify the first three steps in the IMAGINE process to begin program development

C.   Address the questions provided after the vignette

First three steps in the IMAGINE process:

1.

2.

3.

Vignette: Larry is a social worker at a residential treatment center for adolescents who have serious behavioral and emotional problems. He attends a courtroom proceeding to speak on the behalf of Archibald (nicknamed Archy), one of his clients at the center. Archy was caught shoplifting and faces a possible return to a juvenile correctional facility. Larry feels Archy has made significant progress at the center and hates the thought of Archy returning to "jail" and backsliding concerning the treatment progress he's made. Wearing blue jeans and an orange T-shirt, Larry is called to the stand.

Larry is an outgoing person who tends to act in a friendly manner with most people with whom he comes into contact. On his way up to the stand, he smiles, waves, and says, "Hi, Judge." His intent is to develop rapport with the judge. As Larry answers questions, he leans towards the bench and the judge. He speaks using his most sincere tone. At times he raises his voice to make his point. He hopes he doesn't sound like he's whining, but is committed to helping Archy.

When asked to make his recommendations regarding Archy's treatment for the next six months, Larry states, "It seems to me that Archy will be capable of making much more progress at the treatment center than in the residential facility." Larry is then asked to submit his progress reports for the judge's perusal. Larry indicates that he isn't quite finished with them yet, but will get them to court by tomorrow.

169

1. What behavior might be ineffective and inappropriate in a courtroom setting?

2. What are the differences between common behavior patterns in social work practice and the appropriate behavior patterns in a formal courtroom setting?

3. What are recommendations for improved courtroom protocol?

Competencies/Practice Behaviors Exercise 13.3
Evidence, Evidence, Evidence

Focus Competencies or Practice Behaviors:
- EP 2.1.7b   Critique and apply knowledge to understand person and environment

Instructions:
A.   Review the different types of evidence discussed in the chapter
B.   Match the definitions of each example below with the legal description

1.	Documentary	_____	5.	Relevant	_____
2.	Testimonial	_____	6.	Material	_____
3.	Real	_____	7.	Competent	_____
4.	Hearsay	_____			

A.   Statements made to a witness by a person who is not present in the courtroom.
B.   Evidence considered consequential to the outcome of the trial.
C.   Evidence provided by a qualified witness.
D.   Testimony by a crime victim about his injuries.
E.   A gun used in a robbery.
F.   Testimony with a direct bearing on a case.
G.   Medical records authenticated by a hospital records clerk.

Competencies/Practice Behaviors Exercise 13.4
Role Play Testifying in Court

Focus Competencies or Practice Behaviors:
- EP 2.1.2b   Make ethical decisions by applying standards of the NASW Code of Ethics and, as applicable, of the International Federation of Social Workers/International Association of Schools of Social Work Ethics in Social Work, Statement of Principles
- EP 2.1.7a   Utilize conceptual frameworks to guide the processes of assessment, intervention, and evaluation
- EP 2.1.10b   Use empathy and other interpersonal skills

Instructions:
A.   Review the information in the text regarding testifying in court and courtroom protocol
B.   Read the following vignette and one person assume the role of (1) the social worker on the stand; (2) the prosecuting attorney; (3) the defense attorney; (4) the judge; (5) the defendant
C.   Role play the situation and report what was done right and what could have been done differently

> During cross-examination at a dispositional hearing, Bella Wolf testifies regarding her experience in providing individual and family counseling to the defendant (Jacob Vampire). Jacob has been found guilty of having sexual intercourse with a minor. The prosecuting attorney (Edward Werewolf) looks Ms. Wolf directly in the eye and poses his question: "Can you promise me, Ms. Wolf that defendant, Mr. Vampire, will never have sexual contact with minors again?" Ms. Wolf looks shell-shocked…begin the role play.

D.   Write your review of the role play.

Chapter 13 Competencies/Practice Behaviors Exercises Assessment:

Name: _____ **Date:** _____

Supervisor's Name: _____

Focus Competencies/Practice Behaviors:

- EP 2.1.1d   Demonstrate professional demeanor in behavior, appearance, and communication
- EP 2.1.2b   Make ethical decisions by applying standards of the NASW Code of Ethics and, as applicable, of the International Federation of Social Workers/International Association of Schools of Social Work Ethics in Social Work, Statement of Principles
- EP 2.1.7a   Utilize conceptual frameworks to guide the processes of assessment, intervention, and evaluation
- EP 2.1.7b   Critique and apply knowledge to understand person and environment
- EP 2.1.10b   Use empathy and other interpersonal skills

Instructions:

A.   Evaluate your work or your partner's work in the Focus Competencies/Practice Behaviors by completing the Competencies/Practice Behaviors Assessment form below

B.   What other Competencies/Practice Behaviors did you use to complete these Exercises? Be sure to record them in your assessments

1.	I have attained this competency/practice behavior (in the range of 81 to 100%)
2.	I have largely attained this competency/practice behavior (in the range of 61 to 80%)
3.	I have partially attained this competency/practice behavior (in the range of 41 to 60%)
4.	I have made a little progress in attaining this competency/practice behavior (in the range of 21 to 40%)
5.	I have made almost no progress in attaining this competency/practice behavior (in the range of 0 to 20%)

Student and Evaluator Assessment Scale and Comments	0	1	2	3	4	5	Agree/Disagree/Comments
EP 2.1.1 Identify as a Professional Social Worker and Conduct Oneself Accordingly							
a. Advocate for client access to the services of social work							
b. Practice personal reflection and self-correction to assure continual professional development							
c. Attend to professional roles and boundaries							
d. Demonstrate professional demeanor in behavior, appearance, and communication							
e. Engage in career-long learning							
f. Use supervision and consultation							
EP 2.1.2 Apply Social Work Ethical Principles to Guide Professional Practice							
a. Recognize and manage personal values in a way that allows professional values to guide practice							
b. Make ethical decisions by applying NASW Code of Ethics and, as applicable, of the IFSW/IASSW Ethics in Social Work, Statement of Principles							
c. Tolerate ambiguity in resolving ethical conflicts							
d. Apply strategies of ethical reasoning to arrive at principled decisions							

EP 2.1.3 Apply Critical Thinking to Inform and Communicate Professional Judgments							
a.	Distinguish, appraise, and integrate multiple sources of knowledge, including research-based knowledge and practice wisdom						
b.	Analyze models of assessment, prevention, intervention, and evaluation						
c.	Demonstrate effective oral and written communication in working with individuals, families, groups, organizations, communities, and colleagues						
EP 2.1.4 Engage Diversity and Difference in Practice							
a.	Recognize the extent to which a culture's structures and values may oppress, marginalize, alienate, or create or enhance privilege and power						
b.	Gain sufficient self-awareness to eliminate the influence of personal biases and values in working with diverse groups						
c.	Recognize and communicate their understanding of the importance of difference in shaping life experiences						
d.	View themselves as learners and engage those with whom they work as informants						
EP 2.1.5 Advance Human Rights and Social and Economic Justice							
a.	Understand forms and mechanisms of oppression and discrimination						
b.	Advocate for human rights and social and economic justice						
c.	Engage in practices that advance social and economic justice						
EP 2.1.6 Engage in Research-Informed Practice and Practice-Informed Research							
a.	Use practice experience to inform scientific inquiry						
b.	Use research evidence to inform practice						
EP 2.1.7 Apply Knowledge of Human Behavior and the Social Environment							
a.	Utilize conceptual frameworks to guide the processes of assessment, intervention, and evaluation						
b.	Critique and apply knowledge to understand person and environment						
EP 2.1.8 Engage in Policy Practice to Advance Social and Economic Well-Being and to Deliver Effective Social Work Services							
a.	Analyze, formulate, and advocate for policies that advance social well-being						
b.	Collaborate with colleagues and clients for effective policy action						
EP 2.1.9 Respond to Contexts that Shape Practice							
a.	Continuously discover, appraise, and attend to changing locales, populations, scientific and technological developments, and emerging societal trends to provide relevant services						
b.	Provide leadership in promoting sustainable changes in service delivery and practice to improve the quality of social services						

173

EP 2.1.10 Engage, Assess, Intervene, and Evaluate with Individuals, Families, Groups, Organizations and Communities							
a.	Substantively and affectively prepare for action with individuals, families, groups, organizations, and communities						
b.	Use empathy and other interpersonal skills						
c.	Develop a mutually agreed-on focus of work and desired outcomes						
d.	Collect, organize, and interpret client data						
e.	Assess client strengths and limitations						
f.	Develop mutually agreed-on intervention goals and objectives						
g.	Select appropriate intervention strategies						
h.	Initiate actions to achieve organizational goals						
i.	Implement prevention interventions that enhance client capacities						
j.	Help clients resolve problems						
k.	Negotiate, mediate, and advocate for clients						
l.	Facilitate transitions and endings						
m.	Critically analyze, monitor, and evaluate interventions						

Competencies/Practice Behaviors Exercise 14.1
Press Releases

Focus Competencies or Practice Behaviors:
- EP 2.1.1d   Demonstrate professional demeanor in behavior, appearance, and communication
- EP 2.1.3c   Demonstrate effective oral and written communication in working with individuals, families, groups, organizations, communities, and colleagues

Instructions:
A.   Review content on preparing a press release
B.   Read the press release below and identify both its strengths and weaknesses

---

Fremont Street Neighborhood Association

For Immediate Release:
      Neighborhood Association Pushes City for Action
      South Swampland, MO—August 1, 2005

The Fremont Street Neighborhood Association has filed suit against the City of South Swampland for failing to protect adequately children walking to school along East Doyle Avenue. The Association president said that two children were hurt in drive-by shootings during the past four weeks while the city does nothing about the problem. The Neighborhood Association Board of Directors voted yesterday to sue in Circuit Court, charging the Mayor and Police Chief with discrimination against the predominantly African-American neighborhood along Fremont Street. The Association is calling for increased police patrols and arrests of the gang members who frequent the area brandishing weapons and selling drugs to children. They also demand the city close the south end of Fremont Street to prevent drivers from racing down the street. "The city's failure to take action to alleviate the problem left us with no choice," said Chambers. "We are also considering filing a discrimination complaint with the state office of civil rights," she said. Chambers said a rally is scheduled for 10:00 a.m. Monday to draw attention to the problem. Following the rally, former Fremont Street resident and professional ballplayer Sam Malone will hold a news conference along with Association officers.

###

Strengths of the Press Release	Weaknesses of the Press Release

---

Competencies/Practice Behaviors Exercise 14.2
Preparing Sound Bites

Focus Competencies or Practice Behaviors:
- EP 2.1.1d   Demonstrate professional demeanor in behavior, appearance, and communication
- EP 2.1.3c   Demonstrate effective oral and written communication in working with individuals, families, groups, organizations, communities, and colleagues

Instructions:
A.   Using the press release described in the previous exercise, create a series of possible sound bites

> A local television reporter has decided to interview you further about the news release you prepared above. Remember that the broadcast media tend to prefer comments that are short and to the point. Write four sound bites that take no more than 15 seconds to say and that convey key ideas about the program described in your news release.
>
> 1.
>
> 2.
>
> 3.
>
> 4.

Competencies/Practice Behaviors Exercise 14.3
Draft a Letter to the Editor

Focus Competencies or Practice Behaviors:
- EP 2.1.1d   Demonstrate professional demeanor in behavior, appearance, and communication
- EP 2.1.3c   Demonstrate effective oral and written communication in working with individuals, families, groups, organizations, communities, and colleagues

Instructions:
A.   Review the information about writing letters to the media
B.   Choose a topic that has been in the news in the past few days
C.   Prepare a letter to be sent to the editorial page of your local newspaper expressing your opinion on this topic

News Topic:

Competencies/Practice Behaviors Exercise 14.4
Role Play Media Interview/Press Conference

Focus Competencies or Practice Behaviors:
- EP 2.1.3c   Demonstrate effective oral and written communication in working with individuals, families, groups, organizations, communities, and colleagues
- EP 2.1.10a   Substantively and affectively prepare for action with individuals, families, groups, organizations, and communities

Instructions:
A.   Review the information about working with the media, especially media interviews.
B.   Read the vignette below and role play an interview with reporters. Several class members will play the roles of reporters.

A press conference has been set up and all the reporters are just waiting to charge at you with their shouted questions. You are advocating for the 18th Street Take Back the Night Association because they are threatening to sue the city of Lillywhite for failing to adequately protect the young girls walking to school along 18th street. Two young girls were raped and killed during the past four weeks, and the city does nothing about the problem. The predominantly Latino neighborhood along this street is becoming increasingly violent. The police unofficially refuse to patrol this area and the fire department and paramedics say they have damage to their equipment every time they are called in to that neighborhood. Something has to be done quickly before it becomes an all-out riot zone. Let the press conference/interview begin…

C.   What did you learn from this role play? What types of interpersonal skills were used, or should have been used? What type of preparation was needed before this press conference?

Chapter 14 Competencies/Practice Behaviors Exercises Assessment:

Name: _____ **Date:** _____

Supervisor's Name: _____

Focus Competencies/Practice Behaviors:
- EP 2.1.1d   Demonstrate professional demeanor in behavior, appearance, and communication
- EP 2.1.3c   Demonstrate effective oral and written communication in working with individuals, families, groups, organizations, communities, and colleagues
- EP 2.1.10a   Substantively and affectively prepare for action with individuals, families, groups, organizations, and communities

Instructions:

A.   Evaluate your work or your partner's work in the Focus Competencies/Practice Behaviors by completing the Competencies/Practice Behaviors Assessment form below

B.   What other Competencies/Practice Behaviors did you use to complete these Exercises? Be sure to record them in your assessments

1.	I have attained this competency/practice behavior (in the range of 81 to 100%)
2.	I have largely attained this competency/practice behavior (in the range of 61 to 80%)
3.	I have partially attained this competency/practice behavior (in the range of 41 to 60%)
4.	I have made a little progress in attaining this competency/practice behavior (in the range of 21 to 40%)
5.	I have made almost no progress in attaining this competency/practice behavior (in the range of 0 to 20%)

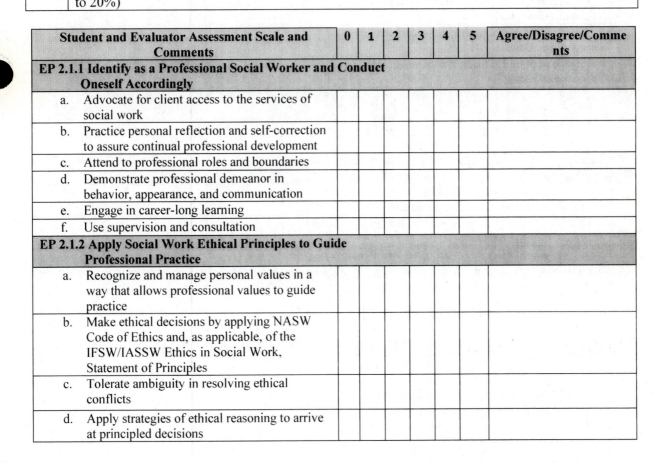

Student and Evaluator Assessment Scale and Comments	0	1	2	3	4	5	Agree/Disagree/Comments
EP 2.1.1 Identify as a Professional Social Worker and Conduct Oneself Accordingly							
a. Advocate for client access to the services of social work							
b. Practice personal reflection and self-correction to assure continual professional development							
c. Attend to professional roles and boundaries							
d. Demonstrate professional demeanor in behavior, appearance, and communication							
e. Engage in career-long learning							
f. Use supervision and consultation							
EP 2.1.2 Apply Social Work Ethical Principles to Guide Professional Practice							
a. Recognize and manage personal values in a way that allows professional values to guide practice							
b. Make ethical decisions by applying NASW Code of Ethics and, as applicable, of the IFSW/IASSW Ethics in Social Work, Statement of Principles							
c. Tolerate ambiguity in resolving ethical conflicts							
d. Apply strategies of ethical reasoning to arrive at principled decisions							

EP 2.1.3 Apply Critical Thinking to Inform and Communicate Professional Judgments						
a. Distinguish, appraise, and integrate multiple sources of knowledge, including research-based knowledge and practice wisdom						
b. Analyze models of assessment, prevention, intervention, and evaluation						
c. Demonstrate effective oral and written communication in working with individuals, families, groups, organizations, communities, and colleagues						
EP 2.1.4 Engage Diversity and Difference in Practice						
a. Recognize the extent to which a culture's structures and values may oppress, marginalize, alienate, or create or enhance privilege and power						
b. Gain sufficient self-awareness to eliminate the influence of personal biases and values in working with diverse groups						
c. Recognize and communicate their understanding of the importance of difference in shaping life experiences						
d. View themselves as learners and engage those with whom they work as informants						
EP 2.1.5 Advance Human Rights and Social and Economic Justice						
a. Understand forms and mechanisms of oppression and discrimination						
b. Advocate for human rights and social and economic justice						
c. Engage in practices that advance social and economic justice						
EP 2.1.6 Engage in Research-Informed Practice and Practice-Informed Research						
a. Use practice experience to inform scientific inquiry						
b. Use research evidence to inform practice						
EP 2.1.7 Apply Knowledge of Human Behavior and the Social Environment						
a. Utilize conceptual frameworks to guide the processes of assessment, intervention, and evaluation						
b. Critique and apply knowledge to understand person and environment						
EP 2.1.8 Engage in Policy Practice to Advance Social and Economic Well-Being and to Deliver Effective Social Work Services						
a. Analyze, formulate, and advocate for policies that advance social well-being						
b. Collaborate with colleagues and clients for effective policy action						
EP 2.1.9 Respond to Contexts that Shape Practice						
a. Continuously discover, appraise, and attend to changing locales, populations, scientific and technological developments, and emerging societal trends to provide relevant services						
b. Provide leadership in promoting sustainable changes in service delivery and practice to improve the quality of social services						

EP 2.1.10 Engage, Assess, Intervene, and Evaluate with Individuals, Families, Groups, Organizations and Communities						
a.	Substantively and affectively prepare for action with individuals, families, groups, organizations, and communities						
b.	Use empathy and other interpersonal skills						
c.	Develop a mutually agreed-on focus of work and desired outcomes						
d.	Collect, organize, and interpret client data						
e.	Assess client strengths and limitations						
f.	Develop mutually agreed-on intervention goals and objectives						
g.	Select appropriate intervention strategies						
h.	Initiate actions to achieve organizational goals						
i.	Implement prevention interventions that enhance client capacities						
j.	Help clients resolve problems						
k.	Negotiate, mediate, and advocate for clients						
l.	Facilitate transitions and endings						
m.	Critically analyze, monitor, and evaluate interventions						

181

Competencies/Practice Behaviors Exercise 15.1
Summarizing the Stress in Your Life

Focus Competencies or Practice Behaviors:
- EP 2.1.1b   Practice personal reflection and self-correction to assure continual professional development

Instructions:
A.   Review the material on the dynamics of stress and stress management discussed in the text
B.   Answer the following questions

    1.   Identify one of the three primary arenas of stress currently affecting your life. This may involve family, friends, significant other, illness, finances, school, work, or any other dimension of your life

    2.   Explain the reasons for this stress

    c.   Identify the reasons why you're having difficulty controlling this stress

Suggestions for Managing Stress

a.   Change the stressful event.
    In a work setting, these may include:
    1.   An inadequate work setting.
    2.   Urgent deadlines.
    3.   Too much work and too little time.
    4.   Controlling distractions and interruptions.
    5.   Problematic interpersonal relationships.
    6.   Role ambiguity.
    7.   Poor match between staff and jobs.
b.   Change how you think about the stressful event.
    1.   Accept that some stress cannot be avoided.
    2.   Realize that the primary changeable element in your life is you.
    3.   Separate insoluble problems from others.
    4.   Examine your expectations.
    5.   Avoid should/should not thinking.
    6.   Analyze your needs.
    7.   Emphasize your strengths—physical, emotional, and spiritual.
c.   Adopt stress management strategies.
    1.   Relaxation approaches (including deep breathing relaxation, imagery relaxation, progressive muscle relaxation, meditation, and biofeedback).
    2.   Exercise.
    3.   Reinforcing activities.

Competencies/Practice Behaviors Exercise 15.2
Managing Stress

Focus Competencies or Practice Behaviors:
- EP 2.1.1b   Practice personal reflection and self-correction to assure continual professional development

Instructions:
A.   Review the material on stress management in the text
B.   Managing stress often means reducing it or finding ways to keep it under control. Three primary approaches to stress management—whether in your macro setting at work or in your personal life—include (1) changing the stressful event, (2) changing the way you think about the stressful event, and (3) adopting specific strategies and techniques to help control your stress level
C.   Read the following material and answer the subsequent questions

Changing the Stressful Event

1. At least five areas of problems in a work context can cause you undue stress which you need to control (Brody, 2005; Corey & Corey, 2007; Dolgoff, 2005; Gibelman & Furman, 2008; Sheafor & Horejsi, 2006). These include:

    a. _Inadequate Setting:_ Is your immediate work environment conducive to getting your work done? Do you have sufficient privacy? Is it quiet enough to concentrate? Do you have enough time to take care of necessary paperwork without interruption? Does your office look pleasant and feel comfortable?

    b. _Urgent Deadlines:_ Do you feel unable to catch up on your paperwork no matter what you do? How can you assume greater control of deadlines and paperwork? Is there any way to decrease the urgency of deadlines? To decrease the amount of paperwork you must do? Can you record less? Are you incorporating too much detail? Are there ways for you to become more efficient in your completion of paperwork? Can you find more lead time for accomplishing tasks and goals? Can you manage your time better? Can your supervisor help you better organize your priorities?

    c. _Too Much Work and Too Little Time:_ Do you clearly understand your job role? Are your expectations for your own performance appropriate? Are you spending your time on the most significant tasks? Or are you wasting time on overly repetitive or low-priority tasks?

    d. _Distractions and Interruptions:_ Are people constantly popping into your office? Does the phone ring incessantly? Do you feel you never have an opportunity to _think?_ How can you get better control of your time? Can you shut your door during certain times of the day? Can you put up a "Please do not disturb" sign? Can you set aside some predetermined amount of time to finish your paperwork? Can an administrative assistant or secretary hold your calls and take messages so that you're not constantly distracted?

    e. _Problematic Interpersonal Relationships:_ Are there other personnel in the office whose poorly developed interpersonal skills continuously annoy you? Can you approach these people and try to work out your differences? Can you ask your supervisor to act as a mediator? If you don't think resolution is realistically possible, can you minimize your involvement or interaction with the individual without interfering with your own ability to do your job? Can you change your perspective on those you find annoying?

2. In the list below, check the events you feel are stressful in your life

Inadequate Setting	____	yes	____	no
Urgent Deadlines	____	yes	____	no
Too much Work and Too Little Time	____	yes	____	no
Controlling Distractions	____	yes	____	no
Problematic Interpersonal Relationships	____	yes	____	no

3.   Describe in detail the reasons each event you checked above causes you stress

4.   Think carefully about events and aspects of these events over which you might work to gain control. Explain in detail what you could do to change these stressful events

Changing How You Think About the Stressful Event

1.   If you can't change the stressful event or situation itself as discussed above, a second approach to stress management is changing how you think about the stressful event. Consider the following suggestions:
- Accept that some stress cannot be avoided. Do you have to worry about every stressor? Or can you accept the fact that some stressors are going to exist regardless and put them out of your mind as much as possible?
- Realize that the primary changeable element in your life is you. Appreciate the fact that you can control your thinking and your behavior.
- Separate insoluble problems from others. If you can't solve the problem, can you put it out of your mind and stop worrying about it?
- Examine your expectations. Put plainly, dump the unrealistic ones. Both positive thinking (reframing a negative event to look more positive) and talking to others about your expectations can be helpful. Try to become realistic.
- Avoid *should/should not* thinking. This limits your options. Are you wasting time worrying about what you should be doing while you're not doing it? Either do it or don't, but don't waste time worrying about it.

- Analyze your needs. What do you *really* need? How much does the stressful event really affect you? To what extent should you let it bother you? Are you wasting time and energy thinking about it?
- Emphasize your strengths—physical, emotional, and spiritual. Could your time be better spent placing greater emphasis on positive aspects of your life instead of dwelling on the stress-producing negatives?

2. Select a stressful event or condition that you feel you cannot change. Describe the event or condition below

3. Describe how you might change your thinking about this event or condition. (For example, is your instructor's grading scale exceptionally hard in your estimation? Can you change your thinking about this issue by, say, lowering your expectations from getting an A to getting a B?)

Adopting Stress Management Strategies

1.   Check any of the following relaxation responses you are willing to try
         _____   Deep breathing relaxation
         _____   Imagery relaxation
         _____   Progressive muscle relaxation
         _____   Meditation

2.   Describe when and where you will begin (or explain why they won't work for you)

3.   Describe what kinds of exercise, if any, in which you are willing to participate (or explain why this approach won't work for you)

4.   When will you begin?

5.   Where will you exercise and under what circumstances?

6.   What reinforcing or enjoyable activities might you participate in that could help you relieve stress?

7.   Who might you turn to for social support in reducing stress?

Focus Competencies or Practice Behaviors:
- EP 2.1.1b   Practice personal reflection and self-correction to assure continual professional development

Instructions:

A.   Review the material on time management in the text
B.   There are a number of elements that cause you and just about everyone else to waste time. Review the "time troublers," likely reasons, and possible options listed below. Then answer the subsequent questions

Time Troublers	Likely Reasons	Possible Options
What a mess!	Confusion, disorder	Throw out, re-organize, file
Hurry, hurry!	Doing too much too fast, too little attention to detail	Undertake less, allow more time, just say no
I just can't decide.	Terror at making mistakes, cowering at responsibility, can't prioritize and set goals	Use decision-making, problem-solving, and goal-setting skills
Oops! Forgot to plan.	Just didn't think, things happened too fast	Take time to think things through ahead of time, allow time for thought
There's just too much to do!	Unable to say no, too much pressure to perform, can't prioritize	Prioritize goals, just say no, evaluate what is possible to accomplish
I'll do it later.	Being overwhelmed, don't feel like it, it's too hard	Prioritize tasks, plan how to accomplish the most significant
There's that phone again!	Can't resist answering, too nonassertive to not answer or speak briefly, can't control yourself	Talk briefly, stick to the main points, offer to return call later
Unwanted guests	Just can't say no, talking is fun, allows you to avoid work	Limit easy access and availability, be assertive

[1]Most of this material is adapted from R. A. Mackenzie, *The Time Trap: Managing Your Way Out,* 1972. New York: AMACON.

188

1. Now answer the following questions

    a. What is your #1 time troubler? _____

        What are the likely reasons for this troubler?

        What are your potential options for controlling this troubler?

    b. What is your #2 time troubler? _____

        What are the likely reasons for this troubler?

        What are your potential options for controlling this troubler?

    c. What is your #3 time troubler? _____

        What are the likely reasons for this troubler?

        What are your potential options for controlling this troubler?

189

Focus Competencies or Practice Behaviors:
- EP 2.1.1b   Practice personal reflection and self-correction to assure continual professional development

Instructions:

A.   Review the material on time management in the text

B.   There are a number of elements that cause you and just about everyone else to waste time. They include (Curtis & Detert, 1981, pp. 190-91; Schafer, 1998)

-    *"Preoccupation"* is being lost in thought over something other than what you are supposed to be doing
-    *Poor Task "Pacing"* means not allowing yourself adequate time to complete a set of necessary activities, goals, or tasks
-    *"Stimulus Overload"* occurs when you have so much to do that you could not possibly complete all of the tasks in the amount of time allowed
-    *"Stimulus Underload"* occurs when you don't have enough interesting things to do—things that hold your attention or concentration—so you don't get anything done
-    *"Anxiety"* is "a mood state wherein the person anticipates future danger or misfortune with apprehension" often involving "worry, unease, or dread" (Gray & Zide, 2008, p. 118)

1.   Which if any of the following problems characterize how you manage your work time. Check all that apply

_____ Preoccupation   _____ Poor task pacing
_____ Stimulus overload   _____ Stimulus underload
_____ Anxiety

2.   Give specific examples of how the time management problems you checked above interfere with your ability to complete necessary tasks

-    What were you trying to accomplish?

-    How did you react?

-    What were the results?

| Competencies/Practice Behaviors Exercise 15.5 |
| Identify Your Problems in Time Management |

Focus Competencies or Practice Behaviors:
- EP 2.1.1b   Practice personal reflection and self-correction to assure continual professional development

Instructions:
A.   Review the material on time management in the text
B.   Below list ten goals that you would like to accomplish in a given day. Remember that goals don't have to be set up on a daily basis. They can extend over weeks, months, or years, depending on the unit of time over which you wish to gain control. In reality, the number of goals you set for yourself is arbitrary. Likewise, the goals you set during any particular day may vary radically. The intent of this exercise is to teach you a procedure for goal-planning that you can use for any day you choose.

Ten goals for _____ include:
(date)
Un-prioritized List   New Priority

1. _____
2. _____
3. _____
4. _____
5. _____
6. _____
7. _____
8. _____
9. _____
10. _____

C.	Now, in the list above, prioritize your goals according to their importance by using the ABC method (Olpin & Hesson, 2007; Schafer, 1998). Assign a value of A, B, or C to each goal you cited above. A goals are top priorities that you absolutely want to get done no matter what. C goals, on the other hand, are relatively unimportant, things you would like to accomplish, but probably never will. Don't waste precious time worrying about things that you cannot or will not do. C goals often get relegated to the circular file.

B goals lie somewhere between A and C goals. You should get them done pretty soon, but you probably don't have time to do them today. Frequently, today's B goal becomes tomorrow's A goal as a deadline approaches (or as your anxiety increases when you don't accomplish something you were supposed to). If you can't decide whether a goal should be A or B, automatically assign it a B. If you're not certain that it's critical enough to be an A goal, then it probably isn't.

Category A, B, and C goals are then further prioritized by assigning them numbers: Goal A1 is the one you absolutely must get done today. Goal A2 is second in importance, A3 third, etc. When you finish prioritizing your A goals, go on to do the same thing with your B and C goals. This process will produce a clearly prioritized plan for your day. First, pursue goal A1, then A2, and so on down the line.

Note that you can prioritize goals in at least three major life areas including diverse areas of your life such as your personal life involving family, friends, and recreation, in addition to work. You can do this either separately or in one prioritized list. Box A below provides an example of prioritized goals using the ABC method.

Box A: Example of a Prioritized Plan for "A Day in the Life"

The numbered items to the left below provides an example of one individual's daily goals, listed in an unprioritized order. They are followed by their designated "ABC" and numerical assignments

Day: <u>Monday</u>
1. Finish Statistics assignment due Tuesday for class......... A3
2. Take Harry to the doctor... A1
3. Go to yoga class... B5
4. Talk to Professor Tuffgrade regarding research project... B1
5. Work at Wal-Mart for four hours................................ A4
6. Write Mryrtle... C3
7. Play poker... B3
8. Clean the bathroom.. B4
1. Clean the refrigerator... C2
2. Go to class... A2
3. Buy beer for poker game.. B2
4. Watch The Young and the Restless............................. C1
5. Call Mom... B6

D.   Looking at your new prioritized system, answer the following questions:

-     Which goals do you think you will actually achieve and which you will not?

-     Will you be able to complete all of your A goals in one day? If so, explain how you intend to do so. If not, explain why not. Discuss when you *will* accomplish them.

-     If you have listed any B goals, what do you think you will do about them? Explain when, if ever, you think you will complete them.   Discuss the consequences of completing them or not completing them.

-     If you have listed any C goals, what do you think you will do about them? Explain when, if ever, you will complete them. Discuss the consequences of completing them or not completing them.

E.   Now specify the respective steps you must follow in order to achieve the first 4 A goals listed above. Six task steps are arbitrarily listed for each A goal below. In reality, you may have more or fewer goals or tasks.

Goal A1

     Task 1:

     Task 2:

Task 3:

Task 4:

Task 5:

Task 6:

Goal A2

Task 1:

Task 2:

Task 3:

Task 4:

Task 5:

Task 6:

Goal A3

Task 1:

Task 2:

Task 3:

Task 4:

Task 5:

Task 6:

Goal A4

Task 1:

Task 2:

Task 3:

Task 4:

Task 5:

Task 6:

Focus Competencies or Practice Behaviors:
- EP 2.1.1b Practice personal reflection and self-correction to assure continual professional development

Instructions:
A. Review the material on time management in the text
B. Review the following suggestions for improving time management skills

---

SUGGESTIONS FOR IMPROVED TIME MANAGEMENT

1. *Understand Your Job and Work Responsibilities.* Effectively fulfilling your job responsibilities means fulfilling them at all levels—micro, mezzo, and macro. Discuss with your supervisor what your job description and specific responsibilities really involve (Sheafor et al., 1991).

2. *Bunch Similar Activities Together.* Try to block portions of time for completing similar types of tasks (Schafer, 1998).

3. *Use a Calendar.* Select a daily, weekly, or monthly format that works best for you, and plan your time on a longer term basis.

4. *Handle Each Sheet of Paper Only Once.* Don't waste time shuffling paper. Deal with the issue right away.

5. *Delegate.* Determine which tasks, if any, others can, will, or should do, and arrange for them to do so.

6. *Don't Do Other People's Work* (Sheafor & Horejsi, 2006). Especially if you tend to have high expectations for the quality of your work, be vigilant that you do not end up doing other people's work because you do it better than they do. View each individual as responsible for her or his own tasks, accomplishments, and failings.

7. *Bring Order to Your Desk.* Organize items on your desk so you can find them easily. (Sheafor & Horejsi, 2006). It is also useful to make certain that information you use frequently is readily available (Olpin & Hesson, 2007).

8. *Develop a System.* Devise some system for keeping track of your deadlines (Sheafor & Horejsi, 2006). For example, you could note deadlines on your regular monthly calendar or use a more sophisticated computer program. Try various methods. Whatever works for you is the best system.

9. *Leave Time for Contemplation.* Even with a busy schedule, allow yourself some "down" time each workday (Kottler & Chen, 2008; Schafer, 1998). You need time to organize your thoughts and evaluate the progress you have made toward your designated goals.

10. *Designate Leisure Time for Yourself.* To avoid burnout, regularly incorporate some leisure time into your schedule.

11. *Manage Meetings Effectively.* Plan ahead and consider following these suggestions:
    - *Start meetings on time*
    - *State the ending time at the start*
    - *Pre-schedule regular meetings*
    - *Distribute printed matter well before the meeting*
    - *Hold meetings in meeting rooms—not in your office*
    - *Don't hold meetings and eat simultaneously*

---

12. *Manage Your Correspondence.* Suggestions to facilitate the efficient handling of paperwork include:
    * *Write brief replies as quickly as possible*
    * *Use form letters for standard correspondence*
    * *Open second and third class mail once a week*
    * *Get rid of junk e-mail quickly*
13. *Use the Phone Efficiently.* Consider using conference calls instead of holding meetings. Outline what you want to accomplish during your phone calls before dialing.
14. *Review Your Weekly Progress.* At each week's end, review the extent to which you actually achieved your time management goals and make changes to increase effectiveness.

C.   Which of the suggestions for changing your behavior mentioned above would be useful for you? Explain the reasons why each would be useful and how you plan to implement the change

---

Competencies/Practice Behaviors Exercise 15.7
Self-Analysis of Procrastination

Focus Competencies or Practice Behaviors:
* EP 2.1.1b   Practice personal reflection and self-correction to assure continual professional development

Instructions:
A.   Review the content on procrastination
B.   Answer the following questions

1.   Over what tasks do you procrastinate?

2.   What are your reasons for procrastinating over them?

3.   Why do you find them aversive?

4.   What tactics can you employ to control your procrastinating behavior?

5.   When will you begin implementing these tactics?

Competencies/Practice Behaviors Exercise 15.8
Goal Planning

Focus Competencies or Practice Behaviors:
- EP 2.1.1b   Practice personal reflection and self-correction to assure continual professional development

Instructions:
A.   Review the material on time management discussed in the text
B.   To the best of your ability, answer the following questions

1.   What goals would you like to achieve within the time frame of **tomorrow?**

2. What goals would you like to achieve within the time frame of the **next week (Sunday through Saturday)?**

3. What goals would you like to achieve within the time frame of the **next month (30 days)?**

4. What goals would you like to achieve within the time frame of the **next year?**

5. What goals would you like to achieve within the time frame of the **next five years?**

Competencies/Practice Behaviors Exercise 15.9
Role Play Time Management Skills

Focus Competencies or Practice Behaviors:
- EP 2.1.1b   Practice personal reflection and self-correction to assure continual professional development

Instructions:
A.   Role play the following situation using the time management skills provided in this chapter of the text. Include time troublers and controllers, prioritizing "a day in my life", and time tracking.

> **Scenario:** Roscoe is the unit supervisor for a county department of social services. There has been a hiring freeze for two years now and the case loads are getting astronomically large. You know your workers are getting very frustrated and you are afraid they will burn-out.
>
> Two of the workers, Dwight and Michael are especially worrisome. You notice that they seem to be rather disorganized and they appear to be spending an inordinate amount of time on trivial matters and then fall behind on major deadlines.

You decide that it is time for a time-management refresher course. You figure if it works for these two, then it will work for the rest of the unit workers.

What would you do for Dwight and Michael?

1.   What time management skills worked best?

2.   Which of these skills do you use now?

3.   Do you think time management skills training should be an essential tool in all social work agencies? Why or why not?

Chapter 15 Competencies or Practice Behaviors Exercises Assessment:

Name: _____ **Date:** _____

Supervisor's Name: _____

Focus Competencies/Practice Behaviors:
- EP 2.1.1b   Practice personal reflection and self-correction to assure continual professional development

Instructions:

A.   Evaluate your work or your partner's work in the Focus Competencies/Practice Behaviors by completing the Competencies/Practice Behaviors Assessment form below

B.   What other Competencies/Practice Behaviors did you use to complete these Exercises? Be sure to record them in your assessments

1.	I have attained this competency/practice behavior (in the range of 81 to 100%)
2.	I have largely attained this competency/practice behavior (in the range of 61 to 80%)
3.	I have partially attained this competency/practice behavior (in the range of 41 to 60%)
4.	I have made a little progress in attaining this competency/practice behavior (in the range of 21 to 40%)
5.	I have made almost no progress in attaining this competency/practice behavior (in the range of 0 to 20%)

EPAS 2008 Core Competencies & Core Practice Behaviors	Student Self Assessment						Evaluator Feedback
Student and Evaluator Assessment Scale and Comments	0	1	2	3	4	5	Agree/Disagree/Comments
EP 2.1.1 Identify as a Professional Social Worker and Conduct Oneself Accordingly							
a. Advocate for client access to the services of social work							
b. Practice personal reflection and self-correction to assure continual professional development							
c. Attend to professional roles and boundaries							
d. Demonstrate professional demeanor in behavior, appearance, and communication							
e. Engage in career-long learning							
f. Use supervision and consultation							
EP 2.1.2 Apply Social Work Ethical Principles to Guide Professional Practice							
a. Recognize and manage personal values in a way that allows professional values to guide practice							
b. Make ethical decisions by applying NASW Code of Ethics and, as applicable, of the IFSW/IASSW Ethics in Social Work, Statement of Principles							
c. Tolerate ambiguity in resolving ethical conflicts							
d. Apply strategies of ethical reasoning to arrive at principled decisions							
EP 2.1.3 Apply Critical Thinking to Inform and Communicate Professional Judgments							
a. Distinguish, appraise, and integrate multiple sources of knowledge, including research-based knowledge and practice wisdom							

b. Analyze models of assessment, prevention, intervention, and evaluation								
c. Demonstrate effective oral and written communication in working with individuals, families, groups, organizations, communities, and colleagues								
EP 2.1.4 Engage Diversity and Difference in Practice								
a. Recognize the extent to which a culture's structures and values may oppress, marginalize, alienate, or create or enhance privilege and power								
b. Gain sufficient self-awareness to eliminate the influence of personal biases and values in working with diverse groups								
c. Recognize and communicate their understanding of the importance of difference in shaping life experiences								
d. View themselves as learners and engage those with whom they work as informants								
EP 2.1.5 Advance Human Rights and Social and Economic Justice								
a. Understand forms and mechanisms of oppression and discrimination								
b. Advocate for human rights and social and economic justice								
c. Engage in practices that advance social and economic justice								
EP 2.1.6 Engage in Research-Informed Practice and Practice-Informed Research								
a. Use practice experience to inform scientific inquiry								
b. Use research evidence to inform practice								
EP 2.1.7 Apply Knowledge of Human Behavior and the Social Environment								
a. Utilize conceptual frameworks to guide the processes of assessment, intervention, and evaluation								
b. Critique and apply knowledge to understand person and environment								
EP 2.1.8 Engage in Policy Practice to Advance Social and Economic Well-Being and to Deliver Effective Social Work Services								
a. Analyze, formulate, and advocate for policies that advance social well-being								
b. Collaborate with colleagues and clients for effective policy action								
EP 2.1.9 Respond to Contexts that Shape Practice								
a. Continuously discover, appraise, and attend to changing locales, populations, scientific and technological developments, and emerging societal trends to provide relevant services								
b. Provide leadership in promoting sustainable changes in service delivery and practice to improve the quality of social services								
EP 2.1.10 Engage, Assess, Intervene, and Evaluate with Individuals, Families, Groups, Organizations and Communities								

a.	Substantively and affectively prepare for action with individuals, families, groups, organizations, and communities						
b.	Use empathy and other interpersonal skills						
c.	Develop a mutually agreed-on focus of work and desired outcomes						
d.	Collect, organize, and interpret client data						
e.	Assess client strengths and limitations						
f.	Develop mutually agreed-on intervention goals and objectives						
g.	Select appropriate intervention strategies						
h.	Initiate actions to achieve organizational goals						
i.	Implement prevention interventions that enhance client capacities						
j.	Help clients resolve problems						
k.	Negotiate, mediate, and advocate for clients						
l.	Facilitate transitions and endings						
m.	Critically analyze, monitor, and evaluate interventions						

Kirst-Ashman/Hull's *Generalist Practice with Organizations and Communities*, 5e and *Competencies/Practice Behaviors Workbook* Aligned to EPAS 2008 Competencies and Practice Behaviors

Competencies and Practice Behaviors	Generalist Practice with Organizations and Communities, 5e Chapters:	Practice Behaviors Workbook Practice Exercises:
2.1.1 Identify as a Professional Social Worker and Conduct Oneself Accordingly	**1, 12**	
a. Advocate for client access to the services of social work	2, 3, 5, 9, 11, 15	2.3, 2.4, 2.5, 3.1, 3.2, 3.3, 5.2, 9.1, 11.3, 15.1, 15.2, 15.3, 15.4, 15.5, 15.6, 15.7, 15.8, 15.9
b. Practice personal reflection and self-correction to assure continual professional development		
c. Attend to professional roles and boundaries	1, 3, 11	1.3
d. Demonstrate professional demeanor in behavior, appearance, and communication	13	13.2, 14.1, 14.2, 14.3
e. Engage in career-long learning	12, 13, 14	
f. Use supervision and consultation	2, 12	2.8, 2.9
2.1.2 Apply Social Work Ethical Principles to Guide Professional Practice	**1, 4, 9, 10, 12**	
a. Recognize and manage personal values in a way that allows professional values to guide practice	1, 4, 12	12.3
b. Make ethical decisions by applying standards of the National Association of Social Workers Code of Ethics and, as applicable, of the International Federation of Social Workers/International Association of Schools of Social Work Ethics in Social Work, Statement of Principles	1, 12, 13, 14	12.1, 12.3, 13.4

203

	Col 1	Col 2	Col 3
c. Tolerate ambiguity in resolving ethical conflicts	1, 12		12.3
d. Apply strategies of ethical reasoning to arrive at principled decisions	1, 12		12.2, 12.3
2.1.3 Apply Critical Thinking to Inform and Communicate Professional Judgments	**1, 3, 14**		**1.2, 3.4, 3.5**
a. Distinguish, appraise, and integrate multiple sources of knowledge, including research-based knowledge and practice wisdom	10, 14		
b. Analyze models of assessment, prevention, intervention, and evaluation			
c. Demonstrate effective oral and written communication in working with individuals, families, groups, organizations, communities, and colleagues	2, 3, 6, 7, 10, 14		2.6, 2.7, 3.3, 6.2, , 6.7, 14.1, 14.2, 14.3, 14.4
2.1.4 Engage Diversity and Difference in Practice	**1, 2, 4, 6, 7, 12**		**6.7**
a. Recognize the extent to which a culture's structures and values may oppress, marginalize, alienate, or create or enhance privilege and power	1, 4, 11		5.3
b. Gain sufficient self-awareness to eliminate the influence of personal biases and values in working with diverse groups			
c. Recognize and communicate their understanding of the importance of difference in shaping life experiences			
d. View themselves as learners and engage those with whom they work as informants;			
2.1.5 Advance Human Rights and Social and Economic Justice	**4**		
a. Understand forms and mechanisms of oppression and discrimination	7, 11		11.1, 11.5
b. Advocate for human rights and social and economic justice	1, 3, 4, 8		
c. Engage in practices that advance social and economic justice	7, 9		3.5, 11.4, 11.5
2.1.6 Engage in Research-Informed Practice and Practice-Informed Research	**1, 9, 10, 14**		**9.4**

204

a.	Use practice experience to inform scientific inquiry		
b.	Use research evidence to inform practice	1, 7, 11	
2.1.7	**Apply Knowledge of Human Behavior and the Social Environment**	**1, 9**	
a.	Utilize conceptual frameworks to guide the process of assessment, intervention, and evaluation	1, 4, 8, 10, 11, 13	1.1, 4.1, 4.2, 4.3, 4.4, 4.5, 6.3, 8.1, 8.2, 8.3, 8.4, 9.2, 10.1, 10.3, 11.1, 11.2, 13.4
b.	Critique and apply knowledge to understand person and environment	8	8.3, 8.4, 10.1, 10.3, 11.2, 13.1, 13.3
2.1.8	**Engage in Policy Practice to Advance Social and Economic Well-Being and to Deliver Effective Social Work Services**	**1, 11, 12**	
a.	Analyze, formulate, and advocate for policies that advance social well-being	5, 6, 7, 8	6.1, 6.6
b.	Collaborate with colleagues and clients for effective policy action	3, 6, 9, 11	3.5, 6.6
2.1.9	**Respond to Contexts that Shape Practice**		
a.	Continuously discover, appraise, and attend to changing locales, populations, scientific and technological developments, and emerging societal trends to provide relevant services	4, 8, 13, 14	4.6
b.	Provide leadership in promoting sustainable changes in service delivery and practice to improve the quality of social services	3, 5, 6, 7	4.6, 5.1, 5.5
2.1.10	**Engage, Assess, Intervene, and Evaluate with Individuals, Families, Groups, Organizations and Communities**	**1, 6, 7, 9**	**3.2, 8.1, 9.1**
a.	Substantively and affectively prepare for action with individuals, families, groups, organizations, and communities	5, 9, 13, 14	1.4, 5.3, 7.1, 7.3, 8.2, 14.4
b.	Use empathy and other interpersonal skills	2, 13	2.1, 2.2, 7.3, 13.4
c.	Develop a mutually agreed-on focus of work and desired outcomes.	3	7.1, 7.3
d.	Collect, organize, and interpret client data	1, 5, 8	5.3, 8.5
e.	Assess client strengths and limitations	1, 5, 6, 7, 9, 11	6.4, 7.1, 9.2, 9.3

f. Develop mutually agreed-on intervention goals and objectives	4, 6, 7, 9	6.5, 10.2
g. Select appropriate intervention strategies	2, 5, 6, 7, 9, 12	2.6, 5.4, 7.2
h. Initiate actions to achieve organizational goals	4, 5	
i. Implement prevention interventions that enhance client capacities	7	
j. Help clients resolve problems		
k. Negotiate, mediate, and advocate for clients	1, 3, 11	3.5
l. Facilitate transitions and endings	12	
m. Critically analyze, monitor, and evaluate interventions	1, 6, 7, 9, 10	10.2, 10.4, 10.5, 10.6

CPSIA information can be obtained
at www.ICGtesting.com
Printed in the USA
FFOW03n0352200814
6971FF